A River Without Banks

Place and Belonging in the Inland Northwest

William Johnson

Oregon State University Press
Corvallis

The paper in this book meets the guidelines for permanence and durability of the Committee on Production Guidelines for Book Longevity of the Council on Library Resources and the minimum requirements of the American National Standard for Permanence of Paper for Printed Library Materials Z39.48-1984.

Library of Congress Cataloging-in-Publication Data
Johnson, William C. (William Clark), 1945-
  A river without banks : place and belonging in the Inland Northwest / by William Johnson.
    p. cm.
  ISBN 978-0-87071-582-2 (alk. paper)
  1. Johnson, William C. (William Clark), 1945---Homes and haunts--Northwest, Pacific. 2. Johnson, William C. (William Clark), 1945---Homes and haunts--Idaho--Lewiston. 3. Johnson, William C. (William Clark), 1945---Family. 4. Poets, American--20th century--Family relationships. 5. Landscape--Social aspects--Northwest, Pacific. I. Title.
  PS3560.O3867Z46 2010
  811'.54--dc22
                              2009054363

First published in 2010 by Oregon State University Press
Printed in the United States of America

Oregon State University Press
121 The Valley Library
Corvallis OR 97331-4501
541-737-3166 • fax 541-737-3170
http://oregonstate.edu/dept/press

for Ched
without whom, so little

Table of Contents

Walking the Bridge Rail

Rocks, trees, and water blur and spin. The banks dance behind my eyes, and the sky does cartwheels until I'm giddy. I try not to look down, but rapids churn and eddies swirl. I take a deep breath and close my eyes. When I open them, the river is all I am. The bridge trembles and the current thrums. The world will wash away. But my friends have dared me. Gritting my teeth, I crouch on the narrow concrete rail, rise, and, stretching my arms like wings, inch my way across.

Howie held the record for distance. He made it nearly halfway, but it wasn't easy. Forty-some feet below, the river surged through a stony channel. The dare-taker braced himself and tried to stay calm as he crept along. The rail was only six inches wide. I never said I was afraid of heights, but my friends guessed. "Don't look down," Howie snickered. "Bet you can't go five feet," Allen taunted. Whoever fell off would have been in for it. Just downstream, the river dashed over boulders and plunged into a hole of foam.

The rail-walker had to stay alert. Before climbing on, he leaned over to gauge his chances. He pondered the current and its rocky bed, took in the brushy bank nearest him, and made a mental snapshot of the closest piling—hand or knee-grip there? He calculated how hard, far, and in which direction he'd have to swim, and reminded himself to land feetfirst if he fell in. Before he stood and got his balance, we conferred on scenarios: If you landed there, you could dog-paddle over to the bank. If you came up there and swam hard, you could make it to the piling—someone could call the cops.

Our parents had warned us about the river. Once I tried wading to one of the islands and nearly got swept away. But the river lured us with riches. Cottonwoods were crow's nest lookouts, and thickets of alder and willow harbored us like caves. We built forts of driftwood and bolstered them with drowned tires or old fish

9

line. Logjams were council sites or places to lie in ambush. Old
lures and bobbers were protective charms.

Often we forgot about rail-walking. We skipped stones from
the bank, played army, or built a ragged raft. Once when I glanced
down from the bridge, something that wasn't the river moved. A
small slice of current had broken off, turned darker, then tried
to get back and become invisible again. Then there were slices
everywhere. They were trout, heads upstream, taking in the river's
news. Watching, I imagined what I couldn't see—bodies of ants,
gnats, bees, or mayflies trundled downstream. Suddenly I was
seeing through the eyes of a trout. An invisible world came to
light, and its layers kept unfolding.

The river was a shape-shifter. It foamed over boulders,
thundered spitting froth, then shrugged and grew calm again,
hiding its secrets. It changed its routine almost imperceptibly.
Panes of current wove in and out of each other, moving and
seeming not to at the same time, as if the rippled mirror at the
amusement park had suddenly turned to water. And the river
was beautiful. Its bed held stones of many colors—brown, olive,
copper, iron, black, gray—and on pilings rinsed in sunlight, algae
clung like matted hair.

The water was cold, and except for the silt of runoff or a sluggish
eddy, it ran clear. Whether it spilled from my hands, dashed
over boulders, or lumbered in bottomless pools, it set the "solid"
banks—rocks, trees, deadfall, and the bluffs beyond—in motion
and made me see double. The world, once so solid and familiar,
started heaving and sighing and wanting to be like the river. The
fixed, reliable earth was beside itself. Sometimes it made my head
spin. I tried to locate a fixed point, like the small dot of our house
on the bluff, or a bridge piling spattered with pigeon dung where
the watermarks of time held still.

One thing hinged on another. Watching trout, I learned where
to find them the next time I looked. When they weren't there, I
revised my looking and learned again. One spring I discovered

10

willow saplings had waded to their knees to drink. In late summer I was shocked to find them high and dry. The next year I learned this wasn't true: it was the river that had surged up, then withdrawn, nearly drowning the willows before stranding them again.

In the fall at low water, I discovered the river had a darker side. In the shadows of cottonwoods, a culvert trickled sewage, and ravens feasted on the carcass of a muskrat. Once in a crowd of driftwood, the body of a horse rose and fell, a specter of the river's underworld. When a condom drifted past, I thought it was a deflated balloon. In summer, bums camped near the abutment left empty wine bottles, burnt cans, and shreds of clothing. Carcasses of pikeminnows—"squawfish" to us boys—they used for trout bait littered the banks, raising a stench that nearly gagged us.

.‿

What the river taught me became a catalyst for later journeys. As I grew up, I learned more—from mountains, forests, and still other rivers, and the people who knew and loved them. These journeys, along with my family's return to the West, where my wife and I were raised, led to the subject of this book: the landscape of belonging. Together we discovered a larger family—of creatures, people, and places—and found ourselves facing a crucial question. In Paul Shepard's words, "How are we to become native to this land?" Each day the challenge grows. When we look closely at how we live, the question is troubling. Whether by choice, circumstance, or necessity, most of us live as if we hardly belonged at all. And much of our culture seems bent on destroying the very roots of belonging.

Seeing and *landscape* are keys in the vocabulary of ecology and nature writing. In this book, they are terms for belonging. *Seeing* suggests not just the play of surfaces, but life observed with care and attention. *Landscape* recalls not just what we look at, but the indwelling life of a place—its history, geography, flora, fauna, and the stories its people share. Landscape is not out there, but reveals,

11

in Gary Holthaus's words, "the way that humans are immanent in Nature, and the way that Nature is immanent in humans." But *nature* is a loaded word. Its meaning encompasses everything, from spiritual mystery to as yet undiscovered subatomic particles. And nature, and its landscapes, include not only what pleases us, but what saddens and dismays—life in the ghetto or cancer ward.

How we belong, and don't belong, depends on the character of our awareness. As the poet Rilke put it, "we never know / the contours of our own / emotions—just what forms them from outside." Another current in this book concerns consciousness and our use, and abuse, of it. Rilke sensed a link between landscape and self-awareness—that nature, with its textures, shapes, surfaces, and colors reveals an inside. It's a surrogate self, a second mind. Whether we call this mind atomic energy, psychic force, or poetic insight depends not on reason alone, but on imagination—a co-inspired seeing—and on how we respect creatures, places, and each other.

With rare exceptions, industrial cultures behave as if nature had no inside. We subvert or ignore the reciprocity humans share with other living things, what E. O. Wilson calls *biophilia,* "the connections that human beings subconsciously seek with the rest of life." As wetlands are drained, grasslands vanish, forests are burned, and mountains are choked by suburban sprawl, our chances for contact diminish. And the inner life suffers too. The more we rely on technology to mediate our awareness, the more we risk losing the perceptual skills of active engagement with the wild.

Emerson wrote, "The ruin...that we see when we look at nature, is in our own eye." Though many decry the loss of habitat and species and bemoan pollution and its costs, most of us still assume that things "out there" exist independently of our consciousness; that our spiritual life is wholly interior, not shared or accessible through the outer world—of trees, rivers, asphalt, vomit, eagles, chlorine, SUVs, tampons, daisies, on and on. Our greatest challenge is spiritual. If the world is emblematic of what we are, then how we see it—and ourselves—is a crucial determinant. We share, and hence are responsible for, not only the earth's past, but its coming to be.

My title honors Marc Chagall's painting, *Time is a River Without Banks*. This work centers on Russia's Dvina River and the artist's hometown, Vitebsk. The painting marries the actual, the imagined, and the remembered. Afloat in midair, a wall clock with a pendulum recalls the artist's childhood home. Above the clock, a large herring with plumed wings recalls the fish Chagall's father hauled for a living. Around the head of the herring, a hand reaches to pluck an airborne violin, and on the bank below, lovers lie asleep in each other's arms.

The painting is the visual equivalent of a dream set in a place long known and loved. It frees its subjects from weight and gravity and demolishes the barriers between human and animal. The dream world is no blur, but both subtle and sharp, like nature itself, which reveals surfaces and depths, and implies unseen energies that inform and connect all of life. Chagall's blues, especially, reveal a spiritual longing through which place, psyche, and time converge.

·⤳

Sometimes when we're fully present, gifts appear unbidden. A shaft of sunlight warms the woods, and we glimpse an animal moving into shadows. A beer can dropped near the road sparkles in sunlight, and for a moment life is charged. We feel something powerful and strange has broken into us. Its meaning is simply that it *is*—a flicker of the wholeness, and holiness, we're part of. The green world, the vital world we feel akin to within, whether from blooms of rhododendron, the wheeze of a dying parent, or the ferocity of a hawk's stare, enters and arrests us. Such moments can inform, and redirect, the way we see. So while this book takes up my family's journey to the Northwest, and Idaho, it also concerns

13

how places, animals, and people have taught us how to belong, and how not to.

In an age of mass information and environmental havoc, how can we reconnect with places that sustain us? How can we bear witness not only to the granitic reality of fact, but to the hidden potency of place and our creative role in it? True geography is spiritual. It heeds land, mind, and heart. This mutual awareness is, finally, a mystery, but I work on the assumption that mysteries are approachable, like clouds at the summit or tide pools offshore, a treasury of hieroglyphics we are asked, and tasked, to read.

Risking the West

Bright-eyed and grinning, Noah toddles beside me. His jabber echoes off bare walls. When we stand at the window and wave at the cherry in the yard, I fight back tears. I have pruned the tree for each of twenty-five springs and shared the Bings with robins and sparrows. When I rocked him for his dawn feeding, Noah would stare at the cherry. He and his mother, our daughter, Suzanne, lived with us then. He saw the tree through a season of its life and the first year of his own. But the movers have come and gone and the house is empty now. Noah is three when we say good-bye.

A four-level remnant of the seventies, our home has outgrown us. It offered safe harbor for a family of five, but Cheryl and I are alone now. The daily regimen of stairs aggravates her post-polio syndrome and my bad knee. And there are other concerns. Lewiston, Idaho, our home for nearly thirty years, is a company town. If the Potlatch paper mill were to close, it would be tough to sell our house. Now, in the fall of 2008, fault lines in the nation's economy are trembling too. I feel them when wind rustles the cherry. Cheryl and I have looked for a home we can afford, but found no prospects. In August, we put our house on the market, thinking it probably won't sell. Three weeks later, to our shocked surprise, it has new owners.

Where will we go? What will we do? I lift Noah into my arms and feel his heartbeat. The floor is shaking, and the ground beneath it. The tighter I hold him, the more precarious things are. We have found a house to rent for the short run and contacted a builder with a plan we might afford, but nothing is certain. If the bottom falls out, we'll have to swim, but where, how? As we drive Noah back to Suzanne's apartment, I recall an earlier journey.

⌣

August 1981

Nine a.m. The house locked and empty, the keys with a realtor, and a for-sale sign in the yard. A few weeks earlier, I had signed a contract to teach in Idaho. We spruced up the house, had a garage sale, and packed up what was left. On a muggy Florida morning, before we set out, our two-story, Victorian clapboard, home to our family for four years, looked bereft. Cheryl and I had longed to return west, but that day the windows were hollow eyed, and memories tugged hard. Even the U-Haul seemed to resist. It was so stuffed, the tailgate put up a fight.

Cheryl herded our toddlers, Steve and Suzanne, into the Honda, with diaper bag, drinks, and snacks. Bren, who had turned ten, was eager to hit the road. "C'mon, Dad," he hollered, as I dragged myself toward the truck. After nine years in Florida, with its water oaks, theme parks, shopping malls, and our beginnings as a family, we set out for the mountains, rivers, and wide skies of Idaho.

Eleven days later, our journey amounted to a flat tire in Illinois, a broken tailpipe in Missouri, a three-day visit with a friend in Iowa in the midst of an ugly divorce, sweltering August heat, and near exhaustion. On a hot day on Montana's Interstate 90, I recalled our few glad moments—a picnic in the shade by a cozy church in Tennessee; the proprietor of a motel in a town I've forgotten, who gave warm welcome to our children and showed them the pool. In Missouri, during a torrential midnight downpour, Steve, our youngest, woke with a high fever. At three in the morning, we phoned the police, and a doctor and pharmacist rescued us. In those blessed times, we felt the grace and support of community.

But during long hours on interstates, miles and worry mounted. At the Great Divide, with its head-turning sweep of the Bitterroots, we were too worn out to care. The sign *Welcome to Idaho* seemed anticlimactic, a diaper stop that turned on a rash of complaints:

"Bren's an orangutan. Can you take him back in the truck?"

"Suzanne's asleep on the seat. Can you keep him for another hour?"

Before we left Florida, just after I signed the teaching contract, came news that the college in Lewiston might close. Idaho's economy had soured and a faction in the legislature sought sweeping budget cuts. As we left the rest stop on Highway 12 at Lolo Pass, while Suzanne dozed in my lap, I replayed a cross-country monologue. Homage to Mount Rushmore and its stolid presidents: *if the college shuts down, we're screwed;* to the buttes of the Black Hills and the saga of the displaced Sioux: *how can we afford both rent and a mortgage?;* to spires of the Badlands dusted with western myth: *if this is going home, it's a fucking nightmare.*

Highway 12 skirted Idaho's Lochsa River, a cedar-lined trout stream whose clear pools beckoned. Weary of fighting semis on the narrow mountain road, I spotted a turnout, waved at Cheryl, and pulled off. The Lochsa water was gin-clear. Beneath ledges of granite hemmed in shade, we waded, splashed, and forgot who we were. For a few cool moments, my anxiety—that *what the hell am I doing to my family?* scenario—was gone, or almost. When I pried a rusted beer can from the sand, its glint was momentarily blinding. A promise or a reprimand?

Cheryl and I had grown up in the Northwest, but left before we realized its hold on us. She was raised by grandparents on a farm on the Colville Reservation in Washington State. Her grandfather was half Colville and had married a Danish girl against her family's wishes. Cheryl's grandparents raised five children and farmed along the San Poil River. Her stepdad was a logger in the Okanogan country, her mother part Colville.

Son of a cattle and sheep rancher in Washington State, my father became a beef salesman and eventually ran a meatpacking plant in Nampa, Idaho. My mother was born to hardscrabble Mormon farmers in southeast Idaho and referred to the Northwest as "God's country."

The day we stopped by the Lochsa, it wasn't farming, logging, cattle raising, or family roots that moved me, but the myth of the West. In Florida, we longed for the landscapes of our childhoods.

But those places existed largely on postcards, in travel brochures, and in selective memory—the West of scenery, solitude, and rugged adventure. It was what held the eastern seaboard's fancy in the nineteenth-century, when the slogan "Go west, young man" rallied homesteaders, miners, and folks wanting to start over. It was the God's country my mother touted, the virgin land of majestic mountains, fertile valleys, wide skies, self-reliance, and the freedom to do as you please. That day on the Lochsa the myth tugged hard, but it cast a shadow too, though we didn't see beyond it then. On the river's north slope, hidden by a buffer of trees, the stumps and slash piles of clear-cuts rotted in the sun.

Suzanne spotted tiny creatures moving on the bottom near shore. They looked like tiny twigs encased in silt. The current eddied back, but the twigs groped along on their own. Years before, as he fished a Montana river, my father knelt and lifted one to show me. "It's the case of a caddis fly," he said, and explained how the insect inside secretes a gluey substance grit and detritus will cling to. Wrapped in its makeshift house, the beetle-like nymph will one day hatch, take wing, and if not eaten or drowned, mate and renew the cycle.

The screech of a log truck's air brakes snapped my reverie, and the present lunged back—long miles, whiny kids, the college closing. As the truck passed, another memory trailed, fleeting as sunlight dancing on the water. The woods of my childhood river—the Spokane on whose high bluff our house stood—flickered back. But the present, its worry and responsibility, was too heavy. The hot day, the highway, Suzanne wading in the Lochsa. I felt like one of those tiny insects groping along, a creature of dull, uncertain purpose, caught in a world it had no inkling of.

18

.ᴗ

February 1982
Eight months in Idaho. So far the college in Lewiston had weathered threats of closure. With friends, we saw the movie

Ghost Story, part of which was shot in the Florida town where we had lived. One scene was set in a classroom of the college where I had taught. I was back in the drenching rain, the shade of water oaks, the fume of orange blossoms and stench from the plant where orange pulp seethed in boilers.

After the movie and a drink with our friends, we drove home and paid the sitter. The kids were asleep. While Cheryl looked in on them, I went to the kitchen for a glass of water. When I switched on the light, I thought I was hallucinating. In the center of the floor squatted a Florida cockroach.

These insects don't tolerate cold. They thrive in muggy places where things rot quickly, places like Texas, California, and, yes, Florida—not Idaho. But these scavenging nasties—roach seems too kind—could easily hitch a ride. This one probably roosted in furniture we loaded into the U-Haul.

For a few seconds, I jumped time zones and states of mind. In our Florida home, I rose in the dark, tiptoed toward the kitchen and reached for a can of Raid I had placed strategically near the doorway. Each night roaches would creep along the baseboards, onto the counter, and into the sink. Legs scuttling, feelers wagging, they scrounged bits of sweet potato, shreds of lettuce, or a fleck of gravy. When I couldn't sleep, I became a seasoned stalker. In pitch dark, I'd reach for the can of poison, step quickly into the kitchen, and switch on the light. As half a dozen roaches scuttled to hide, I sprayed wildly, squashing stragglers barefoot, my itch to kill matched by their frenzy to escape.

We never got used to roaches. Cheryl stomped them when she breastfed Steve in the kitchen at night. One feeding brought high drama. That spring when a windstorm blew them from the nest, I brought home two just-hatched sparrows. They hadn't feathers yet and looked like scrawny misshapen fish. We kept them on the counter in a shoebox where Cheryl fed them baby formula with an eyedropper. One night after Steve's feeding, when she returned to nurse the bird babies, cockroaches were already at work. One

19

of the chicks had died. After rescuing the survivor, Cheryl went on a tirade against roaches that woke the house. It ended with an emphatic, "Fuck nature!" that still resonates.

Roaches gave me the creeps. Their wings are sticky and their abdomens the shape of flattened projectiles. They're the color of dead plant-matter, feces, or boot polish, and I stomped them whenever I could. Staring at that impossible cockroach on our Idaho kitchen floor, I realized I had never accepted Florida for what it was. I had admired its tropical climate and torrential rains, even the muggy afternoons, but I recoiled at miles of asphalt studded with condos and retirement homes, the gaudy theme parks, and, yes, roaches.

I took revenge on those innocent insects. My home was the arid intermountain west, but cockroaches signaled life in the tropics. When the maintenance crew of the Florida college where I taught repaired a campus house, they tore off paneling to discover thousands of roaches living in the insulated lath. The insects poured out in a horde, scuttling and clicking. In that sea of nasties, horror found a face, but in truth the roaches belonged there.

Our move to Idaho was tough because without fully knowing it, we had made Florida home. We put down roots, had two of our three children there, bought and refurbished a house, made friends. We saw ourselves as westerners, but nine years in Florida left sand in our shoes. Like us, that displaced roach tried to make good in new country. Stomping it, I felt a tug of regret. Whatever our journey, we carried the past with us. We had our ghosts.

⁘

20   Our first winter in Idaho, Suzanne came down with a prolonged fever. She grew listless, her lymph nodes swelled, and the skin of her hands and feet peeled like old wallpaper. Tests showed her white blood count had risen sharply. There was danger of clotting. Beyond prescribing aspirin as a blood thinner, our doctor wasn't sure what to do. Each week at the clinic, Cheryl or I held her for

a drawing. Suzanne frowned, and when a nurse approached with a syringe, broke into sobs.

Even as Suzanne weakened, we refused to see her illness as life threatening. But her fate overshadowed all else. Work and chores became a distraction. Dishes choked the sink, clothes the washroom, and student essays piled up on my desk. Often, we forgot about our boys. Bren struggled adjusting to his new school. Steve, whom Suzanne had devotedly mothered, toddled around the house at loose ends. Cheryl and I slept less and worried more. We gave Suzanne cool baths to bring the fever down and took turns rocking her into the night.

"To hell with housework," Cheryl griped. Then her voice broke. "I just want her to get better. She *has* to get better."

"I know, hon," I said, confounded, wanting to assure. In secret, I fought despair. "Let's do dishes while Suz sleeps. If there's time, I'll grade some essays."

Winter tightened its grip, and our toddler daughter, once so spunky and upbeat, withered before our eyes. Her blistering became routine. It was as if her hands and feet flaked away a layer at a time. We trimmed the crusts and daubed her skin with antiseptic and lotion. As days turned to weeks, Suzanne grew thin and peaked. I beat down an intuition that she didn't want to live. In the rocker we sang lullabies, read to her from Mother Goose, and in the morning stared through the window at the snow-swept yard. I uttered silent prayers to a God increasingly strange to me.

One night I woke to sobbing. The house was dark. In the rocker, Suzanne slept fitfully in her mother's arms. I rubbed Cheryl's shoulders, kissed her cheek, and lied.

"It's going to be all right. She's going to get better, I know it." 21

"Do you really think so? Promise?"

⁖

That day by the Lochsa River, I wanted to believe we were right in risking the West; that the caddis larvae linked us to the past, and our lives were part of a larger pattern. But that winter whatever myth we were living hinged on grief. It was the story of pioneer mothers who had lost infants to scurvy and smallpox. The story of white children taken by Indians and never seen again. The story of epidemics that wiped out entire tribes. Suzanne's fever burned on. Sometimes I thought she glowed in the dark. In that black desolation, I could find no light.

One morning before dawn, Suzanne fidgeted in her mother's arms. It was bitter cold. In Florida we had come to revere the sun, but I had forgotten the stark beauty of winter. In Lewiston, behind the house we rented, Douglas firs were white pagodas. Icicles draped the eaves like sword blades, and their beauty hurt. I thought of the needles approaching Suzanne each week. In the night's white aura, the cold seemed terrific, an eerie loveliness that hid a darker truth.

By March dirty snow hemmed the drive. I wondered how many Indians and settlers had perished in the West's fierce winters. The doctor phoned with Suzanne's official diagnosis: she suffered from Kawasaki Disease, or "muco-cutaneous lymph-node syndrome." Discovered in Japan, it was found in young children, mostly boys, but was rare stateside. There was no agreement on causes, no prescribed cure. One theory blamed a virus that lived in carpet fiber. I recalled all the motel stops on our journey west, the sense of displacement, the ache of not knowing where we were or would be.

Another view held dioxin as the culprit. It was a toxin released in the bleaching process of paper mills like the one in Lewiston. The only known treatment with any effect was aspirin, plenty of liquids, and rest. When Cheryl pressed the doctor, he admitted Suzanne was at risk. Kawasaki made her susceptible to Infant Death Syndrome. Whatever happened, she would remain weak for several months, her immune system threatened. We continued rocking and bathing her, went for blood drawings, and fought bouts of wretchedness. In a flower bed by the house, ash-colored sparrows pecked the snow crust in search of seeds.

I had been reading the journals of Lewis and Clark. In September 1805, the party crossed the Bitterroots, from what is now Montana, into Idaho. In August of 1981, at Lolo Pass, we had intersected their route. For the expedition, winter had come early, game was scarce, and the men were near starving. At a place Lewis named Hungry Creek, the party shot and ate one of its horses. I might have read Emerson, the perennial optimist, or found comfort in the Psalms, but being in Idaho, having made that journey, I needed to know what others had gone through, for good or ill. If we were a latter-day Corps of Discovery, how had Lewis and Clark's group handled trouble?

Clark's comments sparked recognition: "I have been wet and as cold in every part as I ever was in my life, indeed I was at one time fearfull my feet would freeze in the thin Mockirsons which I wore...men all wet cold and hungery" (September 16, 1805). Cold and hunger had attacked us too, not bodily, but in spirit. In February—ours had seemed to last forever—at winter camp with the Mandans in the Dakotas, Lewis helped Sacajawea, who struggled in her labor, give birth to her first child. She drank a mixture of water and the crushed shell of a rattlesnake's tail. Within minutes, Sacajawea delivered a baby boy. What remedy would bring Suzanne through the winter safe and sound? What could we possibly do to save her?

By late March Suzanne's white-count had leveled; her blisters still cracked but the peeling had slowed. Not wanting more devastation, I tried to suppress hope. Her hands and feet lost their flush, and the thick ropes of her lymph glands began to shrink. A spark returned to her eyes, and the fever that had ravaged her withdrew.

In April, when most of the snow had melted, I bundled her up and she wandered about in the yard. A forsythia had broken into bloom. She picked a sprig of trumpet-shaped flowers and held them close. "Dear God," I thought, "she's alive and strong. We were

23

right to come west. . . ." Then I caught myself: our journey was beside the point. Whatever our adventure, it turned on trials of the heart. Our task was to belong and be open to what lay before us—a new community and home.

To the Corps of Discovery, our trouble would have seemed routine, but we were in agony. Healing turned on ritual: rock Suzanne, read to her, make tea, pray. We saw to her, and each other, as best we could. Sometimes Mother Goose seemed the only guide. If Humpty Dumpty fell apart, how could we put her back together? I turned a familiar rhyme into a mantra. "Good night, sleep tight—wake up bright in the morning light." When I looked down at Suzanne, she had fallen asleep in my arms.

By the time the lawn greened up and buds swelled the tulip tree, we had ridden out winter. Now we longed for spring. The bottom had dropped out and was filling with rain. Normally you wake from a dream of falling, but the winter of '82 was a nightmare. One morning as I rocked her, Suzanne nestled close. Her cheeks bore a flush no longer fever. That afternoon we searched for crocuses in mud near the drive. Poking her gloved hand through snow crust, she found the world again.

･⸜

That winter we found strength in community. I adjusted to teaching in a small state college, with first generation students, many of whom came from rural farm families with ties to the land. Friends and colleagues in Lewiston brought meals and good wishes during Suzanne's illness. If the West offered scenery and solitude, it also held friendship and generosity. Cowboy nomads, gunfighters, hero scouts, and solo trappers are only part of the story, a small one at that. When Lewis and Clark passed through what is now Idaho, the Nez Perce shared food, horses, directions, and a place to lie down. Without the Indian women, Watkuweis and Sacajawea, the Corps might well have been killed by skeptical braves. Add to

24

this countless families, tribes, and traditions and you get a sense of what the West has been and may still become.

When Suzanne grew stronger, we enrolled her and her brother, Steve, in a cooperative preschool. There, along with other parents, Cheryl and I served as teacher's aides. One morning helping toddlers mix poster paint, I glanced through the window at the northern hills. It was early May. The normally bare slopes wore a fringe of green, and I let hope find me again.

Weeding the garden one afternoon, I thought of the Lochsa River, when Suzanne and I watched the caddis larvae. Something else I had forgotten came back to me. That day, kneeling by my daughter, I looked up to discover insects rising off the water. They probably weren't caddis flies, which are rarely seen hatching. Maybe they were mayflies or lacewings, but no matter. Everywhere I looked, the tiny creatures took wing. There were thousands more that didn't. That day, exhausted and sealed in my own worry, I couldn't see what was before me. But the subsequent winter changed that. The college might still close, but Suzanne had survived and we were in Idaho. What would be, would be. We would let it be, and with all we could muster, go on.

·‿

June 2008

On a warm afternoon, pushing Noah on a park swing, I think of the Lochsa once more. That dark winter with our daughter, his mother, comes back—the fever, the despair. "Stop now, pease," Noah urges, and when I lift him from the swing, he toddles toward a slide and slowly climbs the ladder. I stand beside him, hovering, ready to catch him if he falls. A special-needs child, Noah was born with muscle atrophy and a speech defect. But also with a powerful will and a loving heart. Just three, he embraces the hurt and joy of this life. When a hatch of fall aphids peppers the air, Noah hollers gleefully, "Bugs fwy!" I'm there on the river and here too.

25

Brute Neighbors

July 1981

As I pore over a map of Idaho, rivers race through my veins. So many. Such rugged country. The names sound familiar, as if I had dreamed them. St. Joe. Clearwater. Selway. And carved through Idaho's heart, The Salmon—River of No Return. And now they come in a rush. It's as if the place I left so long ago, known only in my childhood and youth, wants me back. Bitterroot Range. Yellow Pine. Big Creek. Cobalt. Stanley. Cascade. When I say the names out loud, others come to life. They're not on the actual map, but on the one behind my eyes. Cougar. Grizzly. Pika. Nez Perce. Pyrite. Hackberrry. Syringa. Lodgepole Pine. Half an inch equals thirty miles. Lewiston is three hours from wilderness—I can't wait.

July 2008

Today I haul boxes from the basement up into daylight. We're getting our Lewiston home ready to sell, doing last-minute fix-ups, hauling what we don't need any longer to Goodwill. From a half-crushed shoebox, I lift the map my father mailed us years ago. He sent it before we left Florida, when I accepted the teaching job here. An old Idaho Transportation Department foldout, Dad kept it in his glove compartment, and after that it slept in our basement for a quarter century. But our years in Idaho have given me new eyes. The map has become a palimpsest of trails, places, and lives. As memory turns imagination, I re-envision mile markers, names, and boundary lines time has filled in. The map is badly worn, but it marks that early tug of wildness.

Before leaving Florida, I dreamed of an animal I couldn't name. I checked out *Mammals of Idaho* from the library and found that an occasional wolf or grizzly still roamed the Bitterroots. I wasn't sure what animal had appeared in my dream. There were places and creatures, as yet unseen, I carried inside, and a dream-animal I couldn't name. Was that why I had been drawn to Florida's Blue

Springs? Why each Christmas of the nine we lived there, we paid a ritual visit?

Our kids preferred real things to toys. A kitchen pan was better than a spinning top. A teddy bear was cute, but staring into a spring run at a Florida manatee mother big as a walrus (minus tusks) nursing her calf, our children were mesmerized. Cheryl identified with manatees when she was pregnant. Swollen in the Florida heat, she got relief wading close to sea-cows nursing their young. The manatees were wild, beautiful, and threatened. Props of powerboats left deep scars along their flanks and spines. As we watched the manatees at Blue Springs, the dream-animal kept nudging me.

⌣

In Idaho, we finally met. It happened one July in the Salmon River range, at Red River meadow. As the proprietor gave us the key to the cabin we had rented for a week, she said offhandedly, "Don't forget the salt lick in the yard. You'll have visitors mornings and evenings, before light and at dusk. You can take pictures, but don't get too close." I was about to ask what visitors when Suzanne made a beeline for the river, and our host spotted a pickup pulling in to her cabin out by the road. As I hurried after Suzanne, the proprietor's voice trailed behind me: "Whoa, gotta help Archie unload groceries. He's got a bad leg. You folks enjoy yourselves. Let me know if you need anything. . ."

That week we kept creature comforts at a minimum. We allowed for sunglasses and sunscreen, Doritos and flashlights. The cabin had no phone or electricity. That meant no hair dryer for Cheryl and no boombox for Bren. TV wasn't an issue. We didn't have one at home, though Bren begged for one. His friends knew things he didn't—about crooks, cops, and punk rock. His toddler brother and sister hadn't yet caught on.

Near dark Bren stood watch at the cabin's lone window while Cheryl and I got Steve and Suzanne into pajamas. Suddenly Bren perked up. "Dad, something's out there." I snuffed the lantern

27

and Cheryl shuttled the kids over to look. "What's there, Daddy," Suzanne blurted. "Horsies," Steve chimed as Cheryl held a finger to her lip.

Steve reached up, grabbed the sill, and stood tiptoe trying to peer outside. The floor shook faintly. From out in the yard came grunts and thudding noises. It sounded like large, lazy creatures lumbered around rubbing wet sandpaper on stones. Then sandpaper was a tongue, and stone a block of salt. Whatever they were, these animals craved what their biology had slighted. "What had ours shortchanged us?" I wondered. Night vision, for sure. When my eyes adjusted, I made out vague shadowy lumps. The noises came and went, as if tipsy neighbors played a game of shuffleboard.

In the beam of my flashlight, through river mist, shaggy silhouettes rose and fell. Then antlers appeared, curved and elongated, like a fan with fingerlike serrations. "A moose rack," I whispered, and twin pinpricks of light stared back. "Mooses," Steve practically shouted, prompting a "shhh" from Cheryl. "We don't want to scare them." The blat of frogs and the chirp of crickets mingled with their lapping. The moose lounged and swaggered, and we caught their scent. Musk, mange, moose-breath? I wondered what moss tasted like—collard greens, brussels sprouts, Limburger cheese? Bog-lovers, twig-gnawers, the moose got under our skin. In the dark they seemed less like animals than great lumbering cousins. Their lapping made me hungry, for what I wasn't sure.

As we squinted and listened, the feeling we were kin grew stronger. And just as suddenly the moose were gone, their hoofbeats muffled in river sound. In the morning Bren knelt to inspect their tracks, heart shaped, the size of double fists. The salt block was no longer square, but rounded, with deep grooves in its sides, an abstract sculpture moose tongues had carved.

We never forgot that night visit. The next morning Suzanne bubbled, "Daddy, will the moose come back?" "They sounded huge," Bren mused, glancing out the window once more. Just then, there were no visitors.

During the night, we felt strangely connected to the moose. Unable to see them, we relied on the more intimate senses of hearing and smell, and their hooves shook the earth beneath us. I realized I live in a society of watchers used to TV, scenery, picture windows, and homes with a view. I privilege the visual and want to be *shown* a good time. But Red River prompted deeper knowing. "Remember what the crossing guard says at school?" Cheryl asked the kids. At Red River, "Stop, look, and listen" served us well. And the meadow gave rich feedback: the chirp of siskin or tree frog; tang of river grass and lodgepole pine; the cool purl of the stream.

Once as we hiked, I chewed a long stalk of wheatgrass, and the kids were copycats. We ambled along like half-wild cows and calves. Suzanne wove pine needles through her hair until she smelled like turpentine. It took several scrubbings to get the pitch out. On warm afternoons, wasps tickled the eave like tiny winged clocks, and at twilight bats scissored and nighthawks swooped. Steve and Suzanne picked cinquefoil, aster, and paintbrush and made a coffee can bouquet for their mother. At night needles fell like dry rain. One morning we woke to the piccolo of a meadowlark and found peanuts we had left on the porch for chipmunks were gone. Our week wasn't all idyllic—sometimes the kids bickered; one night the water pump quit—but in time, contact with this wild place, and the one in ourselves, grew. It felt like we belonged there.

Early one morning I took snapshots of a moose pair visiting the lick. Their tall, hefty bodies and spindly legs made them look top-heavy, especially the bull, whose rack reminded me of great bone wings. Moose are lovably ugly—say a cross between a hippo and giraffe—but they move gracefully, like horses grazing. "Can we feed 'em crackers, Daddy?" Suzanne begged. I told her we didn't need a moose charge, though the moose might relish saltines. In the dark, they sounded like rowdy linebackers who'd had a few beers, but in daylight they looked noble and solemn. While the skeptic in me said "Baloney," I wondered what we might share. Is a moose face one only a mother can love? The creatures seemed brooding and somehow sad. But they had sharpened our ability to see.

"Wanna follow 'em, see where they head?" I coaxed Bren.

"What if they charge?"

"We'll stay quiet and keep our distance."

As the moose pair strolled toward a slough at the end of the meadow, we circled to higher ground, crawled through a patch of woods to a bluff, and lay in ambush. A stone's throw below us, the moose ambled toward a muddy pond. The bull nibbled willow saplings and the cow waded in to bathe. They both twitched furiously at flies. Bren whispered, "That's awesome!" and for a while we were moose in a wallow.

The cow indulged survival of the "funnest." She rolled over and did a backstroke, flailing the air with her legs. Tongue wagging, eyes lolling, she paddled with wild abandon, a silly, happy beast. Once, I thought we caught her grinning. The bull seemed oblivious—always the male—and kept nibbling willows. He looked droll yet majestic, a far cry from Bullwinkle, the dim-witted cartoon caricature of my boyhood.

What happened in those mud-spattered, willow-slathered moose moments? It's easy to think *about* the event, to conceptualize a rationale—projection, anthropomorphizing, being the poet. But what Bren and I experienced came *before* thought, in waves of concentrated attention, moving from the outside in.

30

·⌣

My education hadn't prepared me for moose. I could memorize, analyze, classify, infer, and deduce, but not really *see*. I was taught western civilization as fact, text, and ideology, not as a felt sense of life. Maybe in any direct way, it was unteachable, a matter of sensibility and intuition, as much as intellect. Work in the fine arts might have helped, but only with long practice, and the curriculum wasn't designed for that. It reflected the supremacy of reason in our culture, with doses of the quick fix. As a result, there were gaps between my life and the life of the world. My education favored words and formulas over direct experience, and so may have instilled a powerful forgetting.

The novelist John Fowles shares a useful example. An amateur botanist, he became, in his words, "addicted to purpose." When he discovered a Military Orchid, a rare species, he took careful measurements, photographed it from several angles, then double-checked his field guide and locator map. As he drove off, it dawned on him: although he'd looked carefully at the orchid, he hadn't really *seen* it. Instead, he framed the experience in the "present past"—his knowledge of botany and rare plants. While too little knowledge feeds ignorance, Fowles argues, too much risks even worse: it ignores creative hunch and association and limits attention to the routine or formulaic.

· ◞

The moose at Red River have not let go of me. Maybe I own a moose gene tired of being recessive, or some vestige of ungulate protoplasm making a comeback. One thing is certain: seeing moose, hearing and smelling them, and rambling where they did, offered a contact impossible to glean from books or talk. Now animals who wade and tread the mossy woods aren't mere facts but part of my sense of the world. That a moose snout looks like a waterlogged stump is no poet's fancy, but a truth born of seeing.

Surfaces betray interiors. A mature bull tips the scales at fourteen hundred pounds, three times the weight of an adult black bear, and can stand seven-and-a-half feet high at the shoulders. Call it a neutral fact. But observe moose close up and feel what the body knows. A mature male's antlers can touch a basketball rim, a fact

31

my kids now appreciate. Moose like wet country, but watch them closely and it's as if they wade through air, a slow, rhythmical plodding, like a long-distance swimmer on a country walk. When a bull wades into eight feet of lake water, skimming duckweed off the surface, it's like a giant fur-bearing Shop-Vac. Wade deep enough, slurp, and you're a moose feeding. Absurd. But don't think about it. Try it and see.

Humans aren't moose, but we can suck, smell, plod, swim, and nibble. We say a dog thinks with its nose, but can we imagine it? My Saint Bernard, God save him, never gingerly sniffed anything. He plunged his whole face into the most disgusting entrée. It's unlikely that moose communicate symbolically, but neither do civilized folk think with their sniffers. There are exceptions, depending on training, discipline, and habit. A traditional Native American hunter could hear and smell an animal on the wind. He sensed the difference in the footfall of bear, cougar and deer. In the winter woods, Thoreau could smell pipe smoke a mile away.

Many animals commune and threaten by scent, through glandular secretions dimly understood, called pheromones. To a creature nosing around like this, the world isn't a set of objects but a flood of odors, a sensorium with many flavors. When a bull moose licks a cow in estrus, an organ on the roof of his mouth tells him whether or not she's ovulating. And the bull's dewlap, a tuft of fur dangling from its chin, soaks up the odor of urine and musk so the cow smells sweet love. Maybe this is why a bull indulges chinning—laying its head on a cow's rump. A moose version of necking?

The wallow is an earthy boudoir. Before a bull mates, it tramples the dirt, urinates on it, and afterwards takes turns with the cow rolling in gumbo. It's a get-down-and-dirty approach, a total immersion in the earthiness of loving, like honeymooning in a latrine. Humans have developed more refined habits, though occasionally we indulge in throwbacks like mud wrestling.

32

One afternoon at Red River, a child yelled for dear life. We ran onto the cabin porch to see Steve racing toward us. He and Suzanne had been sitting on the bridge tossing pebbles in the stream. As he sobbed in Cheryl's arms, Steve said a moose had charged him. Had our night watches frightened him? Had I overdone it with warnings? I scanned the meadow with field glasses but saw only a pair of deer. Steve's imagination may have produced a felt fact. He believed what he saw, the way an animal would, unburdened, and unprotected, by thought.

The next day at a hatchery near Red River Ranger Station, we watched Chinook salmon in a holding tank. The fish lay near the bottom like large elongated stones. A young biologist asked Suzanne if she'd like to hold a minnow. "O.K," she grinned, glancing at me for reassurance. He dipped a net into the fry pond, hauled out a fingerling, and tipped it into her cupped hands. When it flipped, she giggled. It was cloudy that day. When I splashed water into her hands, sun broke through, and the fingerling slipped through rainbow mist back into the pond.

·~

One morning as I walked the meadow, I felt looked at. I glanced around but saw nothing unusual. Was I predisposed for an encounter, "see-feeling," or "feel-seeing" what I sensed but didn't recognize? I stood quietly and slowed my breathing. Pines hemmed the meadow with a dark silence, and willows near the river were stone still. There wasn't a stitch of wind. After several minutes passed, I glanced across the stream. A bull moose stood facing me, maybe twenty yards away. I had taken it for a rock or bush, or not taken it at all. Clearly, I felt the moose before I saw it. Had some before-unacknowledged field of contact joined us, some extrasensory link? Or were my senses more subtle instruments than I knew? The bull's nostrils twitched and his chest quaked. When his ears went flat, I thought he had my scent. Was he curious, excited, afraid? Did he feel a buzz too? When he rambled off, I was on high alert, as if I had taken a megavitamin. My senses were acute. Everything—the tang of pine pollen, the rustle of grass or drone of a fly—seemed intense, as if the air was charged.

Thinking was beside the point. First, I had to know with animal abandon, the way Bren and I wallowed with that cow and nibbled with that bull. Compared to a moose nose, mine is fickle. I can tune in on fresh-brewed espresso, but moose pheromones? A friend who hunts told me he thinks like a deer. Then he caught himself. "It isn't really thinking, more like a knowing feeling, a bodily awareness."

In *The Maine Woods* Thoreau describes a moose hunt he took with Joe Polis, a Penobscot Indian guide. When the Indian couldn't, or wouldn't, answer questions about how he hunted or found his way in the woods, Thoreau puzzled over it, then offered this observation:

> *It appeared as if the sources of information were so various that he did not give a distinct, conscious attention to any one, and so could not readily refer to any when questioned about it, but he found his way very much as an animal does. Perhaps what is commonly called instinct in the animal, in this case is merely a sharpened and educated sense.*

For Polis, information came not just in discrete bits, but as a field of impressions. He gleaned things both subtle and dense. Polis's expertise was intuitive, reinforced by training and practice. He learned from his elders, from the landscape, plants and creatures, and trusted what his body told him. In effect his body *was* the world. His mind trailed his senses like a drift net. He didn't have to think *about* things, but instead, *became* them. Or maybe the woods thought *him*. Polis bore an ancient wisdom, and Thoreau knew it. In our own time, with its environmental and spiritual strife, Thoreau's last words, "Moose ... Indian," are prophetic. They bear the weight of elegy.

In the lobby of a Sun Valley motel, mounted at standing height, the torso of a bull moose commands attention. At first glance, I was chagrined. The moose seemed out of place, a trophy in the land of tourists, trendy gift shops, galleries, restaurants, and ski resorts. But the longer I looked, the more woodsy I felt. The torso was massive, the size of an old-growth stump, and the breadth of its rack approached six feet, the wingspan of a mature golden eagle. Even in effigy the moose was daunting. I felt dwarfed by its size. Posed on the alert, it stared straight ahead. Its nostrils were six-inch paisley-shaped slits, large enough to hold a golf ball, reminders that moose are nearsighted and rely primarily on scent for their bearings. A moose detects odors too subtle for civilized folks to catch, unless they have the nose of a Joe Polis.

A consumer society turns wildlife into décor. Moose silhouettes adorn countless motel rooms. As knickknacks go, moose are cute but odd, an ungulate version of Goofy. We can be in the woods comfortably with HBO, at a safe distance, both physically and psychically, from the actual wild and its creatures. Yet pondering moose, or other wild things, may bring forth an instinct more primal than the need for comfort in rooms not our own. Our common expressions betray us. When real danger has passed, we say we're out of the woods.

Sometimes when Cheryl and I hike in damp, shadowy forest, we glance at each other. One will say, "This feels like moose." Maybe we saw willow limbs ragged and torn, a trampled mattress of grass or heart-shaped prints. Maybe we smelled musk or moose piss, noticed tracks in snow or nuggetlike droppings. Maybe we took an instinctive, half-educated guess, saw nothing at all, or got a hunch that came before thought. Moose is from the Algonquin, eater of twigs. What kind of thinking can approach that otherness? How long must we stand and look?

35

Our last morning at Red River, Bren rose early. He wandered into the yard, knelt by the salt block, and ran his fingers through the grooves moose had carved with their tongues. As I watched from the window, these grooves became molds of bubbles and when the molds cracked, the bubbles drifted off like syllables of a lost language. When the bubble-syllables popped, moose lapped in the dark. Bren rose again and searched the ground for tracks.

The ethnologist, Paul Shepard, argues that Paleolithic hunters were the first abstract thinkers. Tracking prey, you envision what you can't see, and the turn to interior consciousness begins. Maybe we've come full circle. The challenge for consciousness now, as the gulf between nature (as mere "matter") and the human spirit widens, may be, in Galway Kinnell's phrase, to animalize, vegetablize, and mineralize ourselves more. We must practice the discipline of concentrated awareness before, or beneath, thinking, until it informs thinking. But if we are animals, we are also spirits, though here our vocabulary gets thin. When seeing turns on passionate attention (an observing that "serves" the other) it moves from head to heart and vice versa, redeeming our wholeness. Crawling hands and knees to see moose, Bren nudged that promise. It wasn't salt he craved, but something just as elemental.

Thoreau wrote: "Do I not have intelligence with the earth? Am I not partly leaves and vegetable mold myself?" Sometimes, I rephrase him: "Do I own any intelligence not artificially induced? Am I not made of formulas, ads, and the slush of e-mail myself?" No electronic gimmicks or how-to manuals can replace what we learned at Red River. I still hear moose in the dark. I don't think about it, but let the lapping, thudding, and grunting come. The dark is woolen, like furry skin. I smell pine duff and willow. For a second, longer if I'm lucky, I grunt, throttle my tongue, and lift my nose to the wind. I plant myself in a damp shadowy place my neighbors know as home.

Stories We Are, Stories We Become

"I read book?" Noah pleads. It's early evening. He's worn out, but he insists on staying up. Bedtime is storytime. We've read to him since he was one, and books have become his friends. The stand next to his small bed—he just outgrew his crib—is packed with books we read to our own kids. *Mother Goose. Goodnight Moon. Stone Soup. In the Night Kitchen.*

Tonight in my lap in the old Kennedy rocker, Noah points to *The Story of Ferdinand.* I pull it from the shelf and begin the tale about the bull who loved sitting in the shade beside a cork tree to smell the flowers. When he's tired, Noah wants to flip quickly through the pages, perhaps as a distraction. Tonight he *is* tired, but the story holds him. He doesn't slump in my lap, but sits upright. "Buttafly!" he exclaims, pointing to the insect that has settled on a flower Ferdinand is about to sniff. "Yes—butterfly," I answer. And we go on like this, taking in words and pictures, sharing what they quicken to life.

This sharing, mediated by voice, gesture, and imagination, may be the oldest human art. Storytelling is the sharing of culture, tradition, and wonder, all at the same time. We joke about cavemen and cavewomen and consider them crude early versions of ourselves, but one wonders at the stories they shared. The symbolic force of primitive cave art suggests our image of rude, bestial ancestors is a caricature. It says more about us than about them. At some point our ancestors must have shared stories around their fires.

It took Noah and I awhile to finish *The Story of Ferdinand.* His eyes never left the page. When Ferdinand, the little bull who became a big bull and went to Madrid but wouldn't fight, is carted back home, he returns to the cork tree and the flowers. When I announced, "the end," Noah sighed and said, "I tired." He was nearly asleep when I tucked him in.

Later, I recalled stories my parents read to me and others they told about themselves. Part of who I am has come from those stories, and from the tales of dreams and memory. But increasingly we live in a time when stories are not shared by families, clans, or tribes, but relegated to books in classrooms, or discarded altogether in favor of commercial entertainment, where the results are frivolous and quick to be had. Cultural memory—the time-honored sharing of stories through speaking and listening—has been replaced by data or melodrama communicated by machines. Reading *The Story of Ferdinand* with Noah reminded me how vital stories can be. That night as he slept, stories I had forgotten returned to me. Thinking of summer and butterflies, I rediscovered gifts.

Sunday. Mid-August. Mom doesn't wake my sister and me for church. It's late morning when I shuffle upstairs to discover Dad isn't home. Instead of putting on his gray suit and blue tie and taking Mom to the early service and Nancy and me to Sunday school, he's gone fishing. Only this time, instead of driving to Montana, he hiked to the Spokane River in the canyon below our house.

As I loaf over the funnies, time slows to a crawl. When the backdoor whacks shut, I snap out of Dick Tracy. Dad hollers, "Billy, I have something to show you," and I run to see him tramping into kitchen. His ball cap and fishing vest are dusty and his shirt sweated to his skin. Seeing me, he grins, slips off his creel, and sets it on the counter by the sink. When he worked at the Armour plant as a young man, he'd fish the Spokane after his shift. Eventually Montana rivers lured him away, but that August Sunday he got the bug again.

I was a small boy when he first brought home Spokane River trout. My mother cleaned them and dipped the fillets in egg yolk and flour to fry. As the trout crackled in bacon grease, we heard her shriek. Tiny worms that crawled out of the fish sizzled in the pan like rice. Later, Dad learned that sewage drained into the river and made a breeding ground for parasites. Today, he wants

38

to show me a fish, but not one Mom will fry. "Fill up the sink," he urges, and I look more closely at his creel. The fish inside is so big its tail fin pokes from the lid. Dad tips the creel, the lid flips open, and a lunker trout spanks the water, trailing scraps of fern he'd wrapped it in. The rainbow must weigh five pounds.

When Dad leaves to change and shower, I run my fingers down its flame-streaked belly. The trout is glorious. Then my heart sinks. Instead of swimming, the fish turns slowly onto its side and floats belly-up. As I cradle the rainbow in my hands, a favorite saying of our pastor's comes back: "Faith without works is dead." If Lazarus has appeared as a trout, I will resurrect him. I move the fish back and forth in the water, but it still won't swim. I'm desperate now. When I stop praying and am about to curse, the rainbow shudders as if hit by an electric charge. Magically, its gills begin to beat. I'm a believer now—not in conjuring or spells—but in the mystery inherent in flesh, or fish.

As the rainbow gropes around the sink (it's so big it can turn only with a kind of whiplash), I'm spellbound. The fish is beautiful. I wonder if I should take it back to the river. But I'm lazy and easily distracted. After nearly dying, the rainbow probably wouldn't survive longer out of the water. I don't yet know that the chlorine in tap water will kill a fish. After watching the rainbow for half an hour, I get restless and go out to play. When I come back in, the sink is empty. Instead of peering into the garbage can, I imagine the trout alert, alive, and rinsed with alpenglow. That will be my story, I tell myself. The god of the river has incarnated as a trout. But a darker voice creeps in, "You let it die—you didn't have to." For a second, a moral dilemma—perhaps my first—flashes before me. But I am neither courageous nor wise. The story's end, including flies, parasites, and slow death in the garbage can, escapes me. Since then, the ending has become part of a longer story, and that story belongs to the river.

39

⁓

Cheryl and I raised our family in north-central Idaho, near the confluence of the Snake and Clearwater rivers. The geography of the Lewiston-Clarkston valley is braided with difference. On the map, names European and Native rest side by side, their original meanings often forgotten. White names are often patronymic— Peck, Greer, Pierce—while Indian names tend to reflect the character of a place. Down the Snake there's Asotin, Nez Perce for eel-place. Up the Clearwater, there's Lapwai, butterfly-place, and to the south the Craig Mountains (named by settlers for the trapper William Craig), which the Indians called Waha, beautiful place. There are towns like Kooskia (a short form of the Nez Perce word for clear water) and Kamiah (the name of a chief, a term for hemp root, or both). Ponder a map and place-names weave a story.

The fifty-mile trip from Orofino up the Clearwater to Asotin down the Snake takes you from gold rush days (fine ore) to the lives of eel-fishing Nez Perce at the mouth of Asotin Creek. You discover the bonds and severances of history: there are no more eels for Indians to catch, and the gold rush ushered in the modern, and diminished, West. For most, place-names are meaningless, but folks who know their landscapes etymologize. Names are signs of spirit, and the stories they trigger offer pleasure, knowledge, and a foot in local ground. Know a name and you feel your way into what it signifies. It nails history into your flesh.

Where Lapwai Creek flows into the Clearwater at Spalding (named for the thick-skinned Presbyterian missionary who built a mill and tried to turn the Nez Perce into Christian farmers), cottonwoods lord it over the banks. On the park lawn, maple, elm, locust, and pine form a mottled canopy.

40

The fall we attended a Nez Perce powwow, the sky threatened rain. When we arrived, whites and Indians milled around tents and display tables. There were samples of handiwork—beads, jewelry, blankets, clothing. Adorned in buckskin, trinkets, and feathers, tribal members young and old formed a ring on the grass. Overhead, a crow grawked. Tree frogs chirred to the pulse of drums. "*Hey-ya, hey-yeh-yeh-ya,*" the drummers chanted. Feathers of hawk and eagle flashed in the ring; the clink of baubles and bone beads, the tattle of bone chokers worn by young men dancing.

The powwow was a kaleidoscope of Indian life: the swirl of colorful costumes, the *tum-tum* of drumming, dancers bobbing under the trees, families with elders and babies. As our kids poked around the displays, two Nez Perce teens stood to one side smoking and a tribal elder appeared in military dress—U.S. Army. We didn't dance outwardly but were drawn by the drums, like characters who had stepped into a story not our own.

I followed my youngest to a display table holding samples of traditional Nez Perce food. When a quiet middle-aged woman in black braids and buckskin handed Steve a piece of dried camas root, he nibbled gingerly. "It's like candy," he grinned. The camas was dry and crumbly. It tasted like chewy brown sugar and was rich in protein. The chanting grew louder and the drums kept drumming. Where were we? Who were we? The answer was around us and under our feet. It felt strange at first, but in time the rhythm caught and held.

At another table an Indian woman wearing spectacles sat next to file drawers containing hundreds of photographs, mostly black and white. She was an archivist for the nearby Nez Perce Historical Museum. As I flipped through some of the pictures, she remarked, "So many elders are gone, we can't catalogue most of these." There was a shot of braves on horseback in full battle dress; of three young stone-faced children in shabby clothes standing next to a log shack; and of a woman in an ankle-length skirt, hoeing a dry cornfield. "We don't know who these people are, so many links to the past have been broken." She hoped an elder stopping to look might recall a face, or a thread or two of story. 41

As light rain fell, the crowd thinned and the drumming and dancing stopped. A few people still roamed the exhibits. Beneath a pole-framed tarp, we sat on folding chairs with other young families. We circled a large woman who wore a black dress and dark-rimmed glasses, whose black braided hair fell to her shoulders. Her name was Mary Waters. A Nez Perce storyteller, she spoke calmly and slowly. Her rich alto drew us in. Her cadences were musical and paced, alternately playful and somber. It was as if she spoke from inside a story older and more powerful than we knew. At times she paused to let her words find us, and gestured, as if we might answer. Behind her voice, beyond the trees and park lawn, the river moved with a hush.

Mary Waters told the Nez Perce story of creation, the tale of Monster who swallowed the animals and of Coyote who entered its belly to save them. Coyote built a fire so the monster would spew out the animals and re-people the world. From Monster's bones and body parts, Coyote created the tribes of the Northwest—Coeur-D'Alenes, Spokanes, Yakimas, Umatillas, and many others.

But summary fails Mary Waters. As rain fell, children Indian and white listened together. A baby slept on its mother's shoulder. A young boy fidgeted as he gripped the seat of his folding chair. "With a stone knife Coyote cut away at Monster's heart . . . he had five knives, but one by one they broke . . . with flint-chips he made a fire; fat dripped from gristle holding Monster's heart and Monster belched smoke, but still he wouldn't die. . . ."

Mary Waters rubbed her hands, paused, and looked at the sky. The rain was letting up, and a patch of blue scored the overcast. She had us then—we were inside the story, inside Monster's belly. "Monster spit some of the animals out and excreted others— Rattlesnake who got his head flattened; Grizzly Bear, his nose; and Muskrat, the last to get free, whose tail was chiseled thin and stripped of fur."

42 Mary Waters paused again, nodded, glanced at her listeners then back at the sky. "Some of the animals died when Monster swallowed them, but Coyote sprinkled Monster's bones with blood and brought them back to life." For a few seconds her voice *was* the rain. In the distance, the river was still speaking. Now it sounded like tide.

Mary Water's slow cadences radiated the spirit of the place itself—the park was the site of an ancient Nez Perce camp. It was a performance we took part in. Along with Mary Waters we were sub-creators. She paused, gestured, and spoke with Native ears and eyes. Listening to a story of creation, we too created a world.

"What are my founding stories?" I later asked myself. "Which do I look back to for pleasure, solace, and guidance?" I learned the *Genesis* story in Sunday school as a child. Actually, there are two creation stories, side by side, from different times, locations, and scribal traditions, left intact, if not necessarily reconciled, by the early compilers of what became the canonical bible. There is the first, younger account, in which, like an all-powerful, all-knowing real-estate contractor, God single-handedly constructs the universe and its array of creatures to his specifications, using the formula, *"Let there be . . ."* Despite the rich cadences of the King James Version, the account is formulaic and general, and that may be why it didn't register on me as a child.

I remember far better the second, older account, which is more intimate, local, and domestic, the story of Adam, Eve, and the serpent in the garden. God himself is a character in this tale, who walks in the cool of the day. The story is beguiling, at times comic—God makes Adam by breathing into a mud ball, but Eve, who is more delicate, is formed out of Adam's rib, as if she were an intricate construction project. In the original Hebrew, Eve's making is expressed in terms of architectural composition. The serpent, like its mythic counterparts, is smart and can talk, though in this tale its wisdom is suspect.

The parts of the story impressed on me as a child weren't narrative, but moral: how Eve disobeyed, how Adam blamed her for it, how she blamed the serpent, and how, as a result, everyone, by some ominous rabbinical conferring of guilt, incurred sin and would henceforth suffer in a fallen, unhappy world, one my mother, recalling Mormon sermons she'd heard as a child, called "this vale of tears."

43

The story was too cruel for me to teach our children. God punishes us for what is only human, even heroic, what any of us would have done—to know ourselves and our world. This God may be loving to a select few, but he's jealous and vindictive—he selfishly banishes his new creatures from paradise ("lest he take also of the tree of life, and eat, and live forever . . ."). The Yahweh of early *Genesis* is likely to inspire not love and tenderness, but fear.

Mary Waters made me want to raise our kids with Coyote, though the story of Swallowing Monster isn't simple or always clear. Coyote has issues of his own—he can be irritable, cruel, destructive, oversexed, and forgetful. But he takes us on a fascinating journey, out of which we're reborn into the world. Unlike the overprotective, utterly omnipotent Yahweh, Coyote I can relate to, especially to his absentmindedness and habit of whim. In the Nez Perce tale, he uses Monster's body parts to make human beings, but forgets to leave enough to make people for Clearwater country. When Fox scolds him, Coyote gets an idea: he dips his paws in the river and from the mixture of Monster's blood and river water come the Nez Perce, the Nimipu, or real people. Coyote has his faults—he's impractical, a cunning cynic—but often, as in the case of Swallowing Monster, he gets the job done, and he can be wise.

I'm thankful for powwows. When I'm quiet and reflect, I hear the pulse of drums. That day at Spalding, the dancers bobbed to their rhythm, moving in a ring. Their costumes bore the feathers, bones, and fur of animals Coyote had saved. Drumming was earth's heartbeat. I would worship Yahweh-Coyote, catch him slinking through a garden of sagebrush near a county road or skulking at dawn through a wheat field, with chickens, mice, or nothing in particular on his mind.

That summer we visited the monument the tribe established for Coyote, a house-sized mound of stones called The Heart of the Monster. In a field near old locust trees beside the Clearwater River, the story, or its aftermath, stands for all to see. My family walked there.

44

The Nez Perce have a saying, "the longest journey is from the head to the heart." With the advent of the Lewis and Clark bicentennial, the Chamber of Commerce is touting tourism, and a state commission is planning cultural events. Amidst the hoopla, slogans abound—the opening of the West, the greatest expedition ever undertaken. But in the excitement, the journey of the head to the heart is often forgotten, as are cruel twists of history.

Why do we celebrate the arrival of white men in the West? Sacajawea, a Shoshone guide and the expedition's lone female, is often either romanticized or ignored. The Corps' primary aim was a quest for empire, spurred by Jefferson's desire to map trade routes for a northwest passage, and they were not the first to lay claims on the country's lands. The British, French, and Spanish had already left their marks. Along the way, the Corps introduced marks of its own, introducing tribes to guns, trinkets, and syphilis, and bringing hosts of other whites in their wake, Sergeant York being the lone, and distinguished, exception. Lewis read aloud a public proclamation that gave Native Americans an ultimatum. It ordered the tribes to abandon their heathen beliefs and honor the great white father in Washington.

Despite plans to include the tribes, some Nez Perce are troubled about the planned celebration. They feel whites too easily forget that the "opening" of the West was also a "closing," which devastated their people. On the positive side, the bicentennial lets us take a deeper journey, not just over the Bitterroots, but from the head to the heart. It reminds us that stories can be both divisive and vital. Some are worth retelling; others need to be revised, and still others put in their place or let go.

The other day at the health club a Nez Perce entered the sauna. I'd been in about five minutes, soaking up steam. His long, unbraided hair fell to his shoulders. I asked him how he liked the heat. "We had a sweat house up in Kamiah when I was a kid," he said. "It got so hot I could hardly stand it. You couldn't touch anything in there. Even your breath felt too hot to swallow. The sweat house was near the river and after we steamed up, we'd run and jump in. Man, it was cold! But good. I never got sick back then."

The man worked at a fish hatchery in Oregon, inseminating salmon eggs hatched in test tubes. On his days off he enjoyed hiking the Idaho woods. He remembered seeing salmon spawn up the Selway River when he was a boy. "That was nothin' like I ever seen," he beamed. "They do a dance—the hen weaves round and round, kicks up gravel with her tail, lays a batch, and then the buck darts in and out milking the eggs. We used to watch them underwater with swimming masks. It was like a big party. The smaller salmon would wait all around, like an audience doin' a quieter dance. Man, it was somethin' to see."

I remembered the rainbow in the sink, the band of promise on its belly. As a boy I had refused to envision its dying. But the Nez Perce man reminded me that life is a cycle. When they spawn and die, salmon, become food for otter, eagle and bear, and for vegetation that feeds still others. That day in the sauna, the rainbow's death became part of a larger story, as did my father, who was nearing death himself and would leave his stories to me. In the dressing room as we toweled off, I joked, "We're pink as salmon." When I blushed, the Nez Perce grinned. I was the pink one.

Others were dressing in a hurry—businessmen, bankers, mill workers—some heading home, others to bars. The Indian kept his distance. Maybe, outside of work, whites didn't often speak to him. Maybe he was quiet in public, a trait I'd noticed in Indians of various tribes. It may have been a guarded pose, but it felt genuine. The aura of hurry and assertion I see in many of my friends, and in myself, seemed alien to him. After drying off, he sat on a bench, wove his hair into one long braid, wrapped a towel on his head like a turban, and closed his eyes, at home with himself. He breathed slowly and took his time, sitting quietly, like a wise otter, content after swimming in a warm summer river.

August. Dog-day heat. We pack a cooler with sandwiches, pop, and beer, grab towels and beach toys, get the young ones into swimsuits, bungee tire tubes to the car, and hit the road. We'll let whim decide which beach to choose. By the time we're ten miles up the Clearwater, Steve's asleep, Suzanne wants a pop, and Bren has peeled open the window and turned his arm into a wing. When I leave the highway, we bounce along a gravel road and park beside a trestle in the shade of a venerable cottonwood.

To get to the beach we hike single file down a rocky switchback snagged with thistle and cheat. Our goal is a creek mouth we'll ford to claim the sandbar beyond. Observers would have seen a clumsy parade. For starters, we're all wearing flip-flops: thorns poke, rocks jut, cheat gets stuck between our toes. Bren is thirteen and eager to lead. A pair of inner tubes slung from his neck, he's a wobbly walrus. In the center of the parade, Cheryl herds Steve and Suzanne, five and six, to a chorus of "Oooohs!" and "Oweees!" Taking up the rear, truck tube on my shoulders, I lug the cooler, stumbling along like an overburdened giraffe.

At nine a.m. the canyon's already an oven. Heat turns bluffs into waves of cellophane. In dry weeds grasshoppers clack like tiny firecrackers. We wade the creek and claim the sandbar. No one else is around, but there's a reminder. Propped on a cattail stalk, a surgical glove gives us the finger. Against willows, cottonwoods, and river, it might as well be a butterfly. Creek rot and algae waft a dry stench. Cattails click in the breeze.

After dispensing a round of Pepsi, I cut willows for a lean-to. Cheryl spreads beach towels and lathers the kids with Coppertone. Bren wades in looking for stones to skip, and Steve and Suzanne waddle off with buckets and shovels. Soon Cheryl and I flirt with our novels. Between paragraphs, we watch the kids then watch the river.

The world starts to breathe. An eddy slubs over stones; rapids prattle then drown in a roar. We're in a time-space warp where

47

earth's no longer solid. From the side of my eye, bluffs stagger toward the river, try to stand still, almost do, then stagger off again, defying gravity. They lose their density, like clouds that can't contain themselves.

Burnt basalt, hackberry, and biscuitroot form a mosaic—burnt umber, gray-black and yellow, the shades blurred and precise, ragged and smooth. Time is deep breathing, and the river floods our senses.

> *A deer-fly nips my cheek. I jump from my skin then smack myself back.*
> *Tree-frog cheeps and magpie squabbles.*
> *On the trestle, in brash white letters, the two-syllable American name of God.*

Bushwhacking through chest-high grass near the beach, I surprise two garter snakes twined in a love knot. As the ground vibrates, the knot loosens. When they separate, the snakes freeze, as if paralyzed, then uncouple and slither slowly into the grass. Perhaps they're still giddy. If it's funny, why do I shiver? Have I inflicted *Serpentes coitus interruptus*, foiled a clutch of snake eggs or subverted cold-blooded pleasure? Were the snakes going on automatic, or following their bliss? Can I be as earth-intimate as a snake? Serpents were once wise gods and the tongues of oracles, though the snake in Eden got demoted. Today I warm to snake love. It's good to know we share this place. We carry snake genes too.

"How 'bout we float the rapid?" I beckon Steve. It looks safe enough, a sluicebox of moderate waves that roller coaster some two hundred yards down to the highway bridge. When he nods, I straddle an inner tube and he plops into my lap. We shove off, the current takes hold, and I realize how unbelievably stupid I am. We're not wearing life jackets and Steve can't swim. "Shit," I curse silently, but the river has us now. I hunker down, hold Steve close, and try to focus. The ride lasts only minutes, but it takes forever.

48

Afterwards when Steve grins, I don't tell him I'm an idiot. Just now, he's proud of himself. "You're a brave kid," I say, "no doubt about it," and salute. As we roll the tube up the rocky bank, there's a knot in my gut. Someday soon, I'll mention life jackets.

All day we lounge, swim, and sip. We've forgotten to bring an opener, so I attack a bottle cap with my teeth then revert to a Popsicle stick. If we stayed for good, we'd become scavengers—eat the river's body, drink its blood, and become host to local spirits, including parasites, like the maggots churning in a sucker carcass upstream—thankfully, just far enough.

At twilight, the kids fetch kindling. We make a fire and roast marshmallows on willow twigs Bren has cut. To the west, Arcturus hangs like a pendant on an invisible chain. Gnats stitch the air with humming, and just-hatched moths flutter to their night haunts. On the highway across the river, headlights stagger through locust trees as the day winds down.

As I drive home, sand scritches my toes. In back, sprawled under beach towels, our three are asleep. "River time is no time," Cheryl yawns. "We're wiped out, in a good way." When we get home, Bren wanders downstairs, turns on the stereo, and flips through *Sports Illustrated*. Cheryl and I herd Steve and Suzanne to the bathroom for showers. After a snack of milk and leftover sandwiches, we tuck them in.

As I rinse our suits in the tub, a rivulet of sand trickles toward the drain. One day, long after it forgets us, it will reach the sea, part of a larger story. One day when we're sand ourselves, maybe we'll remember, and the story will be part of another, and another, and though their fires have died, the stars will look down to read them.

49

The Floating World

A river trip is latter-day *samsara*. A Sanskrit word, it means "running together" and in Buddhist thought suggests bondage to the endless round of birth and rebirth. But when I'm on the river, I believe the word has a flip side. As you eddy, bounce, and glide downstream, you abandon asphalt and straight lines, and give yourself to folds and layers of current. You lose the jangle of phones and the gruff of traffic, and take on the thunder of rapids, a gull's cry, and the creak of an oarlock short of oil. As you drift beneath bluffs hemmed with hackberry and thistle, life is the way of water. It yawns, belches, gargles, and chuckles, and when rapids smash into boulders, it roars like God. With luck and and practice, you lose yourself and get reborn as flow.

But river-luck requires preparation: patch kits of plastic and glue for the tear in your neoprene raft; Banana Boat sunblock (ideally, Ultra-30); lightweight, waterproof clothing—Gore-Tex, say, or light-colored nylon; coolers (gotta eat and drink); a waterproof duffel bag for extra clothing; and if you're an amateur like me, but want to run technical water, a friend with savvy, who knows how to wield an oar for five hours a day and read a hump of current, a low crease in a run, or froth that turns into an avalanche of foam.

Some prefer a tourist float. Choose an outfitter, book a trip, pay in advance, and let serfs handle the details (getting permits; rowing; buying food and preparing meals; handling and disposing of waste). For the latter there are composting toilets, but my floating friends use a sack of lime and an old army ammo case they call the Rocket Box.

I prefer a low-tech float with ordinary river lovers, rats preferably. Say a fund-raiser put on by a conservation group, a low-budget parks-and-rec affair, or if you're foolish or courageous enough, a go-it-alone venture. Take the family, if you dare. And if they meet basic requirements—can swim, pull themselves back into a raft, and navigate rapids butt-first wearing a life jacket. Clutching a ring grip as you tackle a class five behemoth, you get to know yourself.

We've floated Idaho's lower Salmon several times. From the town of Riggins, it winds sixty odd miles through rugged desert canyon to join the Snake. Our first trip included twelve floaters and four boat-people (river slang for rowers and guides). On a warm July morning, in an old schoolbus, we banged over a washboard road toward the put-in at Rice Creek Bar, passing through country once home to the Nez Perce.

In June 1877, a few hills away, angered that settlers stole their horses and murdered several braves, members of White Bird's band ambushed a unit of the U.S. Cavalry, killing thirty-four men. The event triggered a trail of tears that fall and winter. Knowing the government would retaliate, Chief Joseph led his tribe—including women, elders, and children—on an arduous trek through the Bitterroots toward a hoped-for escape, but the group was captured in the Bearpaws of Montana. Our dust left a somber wake. When I thought of plumes trailing Indian horses, grit caught my tongue. It tasted like burnt motor oil and the tart sting of pine.

We were escaping, too, not from the cavalry, but from the civilization it helped usher in. What sent Joseph's people packing had, in a different way, now sent us. We fled not political oppression, but suburban and urban routine, with their artificial environments and neglect of wild things.

At Rice Creek Bar, we unloaded the trailer, rigged the rafts with frames, and packed our gear into a supply raft. The clear, cold river beckoned. Stitched with prickly pear, volcanic formations were stark yet beautiful. Floating, rowing, and swimming were the order of the day. The junk of civilization—disposable cameras, portable radios, rubber sandals, polarized sunglasses, waterproof clothing, low-calorie snacks and energy drinks, all of which we'd brought in abundance, seemed like overkill (we *were* thankful for tinted glasses, sunscreen, and drinking water).

51

As we rigged up the rafts, some tried to break the ice. "Last one in has to row." "Yer gonna be a lobster without Coppertone 45." Others were silent, wondering what the river held in store. On the verge of adolescence, Suzanne and Steve weren't sure how to fit in or whether they wanted to. Cheryl seemed quiet and composed. I too felt a singular inward turn. Chitchat seemed a cliché amidst the rugged beauty of the canyon.

Ahead lay many miles of river. If the veneer of civilization were actually to peel off, what would we find? The morning was warm, the sky clear, and the river sparkled with sunlight. When the first boatman shoved off and snapped the oars into locks, my pulse quickened. Cotter pins clicked against the murmur of current.

⤳

Before we launched, as I rubbed sunscreen on Suzanne's shoulders, a cry rose across the river: *ka-kai . . . ka-ka-kai!* What looked like an old cabin stood mostly hidden in brush and hackberry. For a long minute, I was back in Florida, at De León Springs, the fountain of youth, now tourist attraction complete with restaurant, concession, and swimming pool. Perched in a water oak, a male peacock spread its lavish fan. On panes of emerald, sequins of lapis lazuli became wild eyes.

From limestone caverns underground, the spring surges into a large pool. Ponce de León believed the water held restorative powers, a dream that still informs ads for cosmetics, research in cryonics, or hoopla for the rapture. Long before whites arrived, Indians knew what it meant to belong. Stories, herbs, and rites honored the past, sustained life in the present, and prepared for life to come. But waves of western settlers, or un-settlers, couldn't stay in one place. Driven by the lure of paradise, that greener grass over the next hill, they robbed others of home.

In Florida, the Spanish routed the Seminoles; in the Northwest, in the wake of Lewis and Clark, trappers, miners, and homesteaders, eventually backed by the U.S. Army, marked the end for numerous

tribes, including the Nez Perce. I thought of our own journey west
and now to this river, a journey that would never appear in history
books. Our challenge was the same. We were strangers here. We
had to learn, and earn, a way to belong.

"Hurry, Dad," Suzanne scolded. "The other rafts are already
in."

Bill, our boatman, was about forty-five, jovial, muscular, and well
tanned. For him rowing wasn't a hobby, but a passion. He loved
the Salmon, knew its history, and relished the challenge of white
water. A month of river running had turned his skin dark copper.
The morning we launched, he sipped a can of nonalcoholic beer.
The canyon could reach 115 degrees in the shade, so he'd need
lubricating. We called him Beer Man. When he wasn't on the river,
he worked for a bottling plant in Lewiston, filling, pressurizing,
selling, and delivering kegs to parties, merchants, and bars.

Bill honored the Salmon with story. "See that prospect hole up
there? A century ago placer miners scoured these hills. Usually
all they got was pyrite, a derivative of iron or copper. Heard of
fool's gold?"

We peered at a dark socket in the cliff above us. On the bank
a boneyard of tailing-heaps sported markers of thistle. Cloaked
with lichen and biscuitroot, ragged ledges rose over thickets of
hackberry. A red-tailed hawk glided on patrol, and mule deer
scampered up the breaks in their stop-and-go staccato.

The solitude of the canyon sparked a selfish impulse. At times I
wished my family floated alone; at times that *I* floated alone. Over
the years Idaho's backcountry had changed me. I found company
without people. One can get social with lichens or hawks, though
relations may be strained. On the Salmon, we joked and chattered
less and relaxed more. We indulged the sociability of stone, the
prickliness of hackberry and the *summer summer* murmur of the river.
Time was current, lulling us to sleep or jolting us awake. Heraclitus
had a rower's insight. You don't paddle the same river twice. Water
level and temperature, erosion and humidity, stones trundled down

the channel, make the river liquid samsara. From a Buddhist point of view, floating affords a chance to lighten the bondage of the round of lives. As you read the water or pull at an oar, the river says, Let go—of worry about your job, your looks, your need for strokes. You respect change without getting caught up in it, though there's a fine line between relaxing and staying alert.

"You feel the changes in your gut," Bill mused. "The river's a shape-shifter. A landmark that looks familiar on one run gets weird on the next or disappears altogether. As a rower you can't afford to relax." The first day we floated five leisurely miles. Rocky bluffs rose like huge burnt seat cushions, and the river formed a seam between us and the wild. We moved through a larger, finally incomprehensible, order. Cacti and lichen, hawk and mule deer, rapids and eddies. How did we fit in? How could we? Was there a way to bring the river's gifts back to homes and offices, the rectilinear grids of our lives? As day deepened into afternoon, the river surged on, slowly undoing the canyon that held it. There was no bucking its flow. On the Salmon time was not in our hands. And as if to complete the thought, from around the bend, came the roar of white water. But the rapid would have to wait. The sandbar where we'd spend the night came into view.

We beached the rafts, hauled out gear, and Steve and Suzanne took a swim, still wearing life jackets. On the sand, the staggered parentheses of a rattlesnake said there were permanent residents here. Near dark, beside a crackling fire, we feasted on hamburgers, baked beans, and salad, washed down with lemonade or beer. Tom, a land appraiser vacationing with his two partners, played his harmonica, and its strains echoed down the canyon. We sang—
"Camptown Races," "Blue Moon," "Sentimental Journey." When a boatman named Jeff doused the cook fire, the coals hissed. We unrolled sleeping bags to the flicker of first stars.

In the morning we launched early, hoping for ten good miles. The Salmon runs in a pool-and-drop meander, with a multitude of rapids (some threatening) and slow lumbering pools. At least that was the prospect for our mid-July trip. The day we launched, the river ran twenty-two thousand cubic feet per second, midway between spring's deluge and fall's rocky hiccup. A sheet of half-inch neoprene pulsing beneath us, the raft's floor glided on the river's ceiling. We slid, crawled, bounced, sat, and sometimes, if clumsily, walked on water.

Civilization peeled off like a wet T-shirt. Shakespeare, Mozart, the Louvre—valuables I had to dump to lighten the load. In time we seemed woven into the place: riffle, pool, and plunge; an osprey's glide; scabs of lichen on stone. But of course, civilization, especially its technology, stayed with us. Without vinyl, aluminum, and plastic, we would never have begun the journey. For rowers the rule is vigilance. For riders it's daydreaming, swimming, and spotting mountain sheep. I watched Cheryl and the kids watch the current, bluffs, and sky. Then the river seemed to watch us, and our official lives drifted away. The Salmon was a liquid body we floated on, or better, a second, deeper mind. Time was the mesh of water and light, the creak of oarlocks, or as we bounced through a rapid, a rower named Christy hollering, "We're gonna die!" When we drifted free, a hawk soared over us. It rode thermals into the high blue, a dust-speck in a river of sky.

Civilization was not all veneer. Under the river's spell, I thought of Japanese printmaking, especially *ukiyo-e*, from the Edo period of the eighteenth century. The word means, roughly, floating pictures, or pictures of the floating world. *Uki* has Buddhist implications—transient, ephemeral, impermanent—but can also suggest lively, happy, or pleasurable. The typical treatment isn't realistic, but subtle and expressive. Think of dawn clouds slowly dissolving or a geisha arranging her hair, with artful ease, before a mirror. The prints of masters like Hokusai or Hiroshige also include landscapes. In *ukiyo-e* there's a sense of casual implication, but also of truth freshly perceived, expressed without judgment or explanation, like the insight found in a good haiku.

I first sensed this quality in a print of Hiroshige's. It's a woodblock landscape in black and white, pressed into parchment the size of a postcard. In the foreground, hemmed with trees, a crag holds sway. The sky is empty but for a wisp or two of cloud. In the upper left corner, easy to overlook, a pair of gulls is about to soar through the frame. The scene is simple, natural, and understated, its effect subliminal at first. Then you notice a small stream near the bottom of the print. Look closely and you find a footbridge, more closely, tiny figures walking. They're so small they look like twigs that suddenly begin to move. The white space registers a stillness that intensifies even as it seems to fade, like gulls crying in an empty sky.

Sometimes everything *but* the raft seemed to move, and we floated in a still center. The canyon was a movie in progress. Colonnades of basalt were a moveable feast for the eye. The thinking I did—not much, given the landscape, the shifting current, big-roller rapids, and watching our kids—turned on the spirit of the canyon, or that part of me it quickened. There were manifold flowings—curves and twists of metamorphic rock formations, wisps of cloud, plants veining and branching, and the river with its panes and seams. I became more aware of what flowed inside me, the patterns of blood and breath, as if I were part of a larger flow, its order felt yet partly unseen.

One fact, carefully observed, led to others. As we approached a big rapid, we lashed two of the rafts together for stability. In the calm before white water, I lay watching gnats hover in the airspace between hulls. Dozens danced on the water's surface, like bits of winged soot taking off and landing again. The river was a trampoline for gnats, riddled with sun-tricked wings. For a buoyant moment, life was a gnat dance. Then the rapid roared into earshot. The faces of my children floated behind my eyes. I wondered about children I would never see, who lived in a far, dry country and would never know a river.

56

.و

We spent two nights on the beach, with a stay at backcountry lodgings sandwiched between. As we rounded a bend below China

Rapid, a row of flimsy shacks appeared, propped on stilts on the canyon wall. One sported a crude sign: *Salmon River Hilton*. Our quarters had no electricity or plumbing—only the main shack where we cooked had running water. That night we made do with flashlights and kerosene lanterns. Cheryl thought she heard mice on the floor of our shack. With a flashlight I searched beneath our cot—old mildewed magazines, stale blankets, a water-faded Monopoly board. In a corner lay a hoard of sandwich wrappers, cigarette butts, burnt matchsticks, and bits of tissue. We had taken up with a pack rat.

At dinner, two of the land appraisers argued about the economy. They each had six-figure incomes and made a living financing the "landscaping" of the planet. When it came time to recreate, they chose a river that still ran free. On the Salmon, the real developer was nature itself. It worked on scales vast and minute, in cycles biologic and geologic. And it worked on us, softening our edges the way water smooths rock. The landscape was dry and silent, but the river brought it awake. Nothing seemed static. If we had climbed far enough out of the canyon, we'd have seen the Seven Devils complex rise like scars. These great stone crags are remnants of volcanic islands formed in the Pacific some two hundred million years ago. In the crash of tectonic plates, they lurched eastward and reshaped the North American coast. On a smaller scale, the landscape relished detail: yellow-eyed prickly pear, a blue scruff of sage, and hugging the basalt like scabs, pink-orange lichen whose afternoon tint turned the canyon into a vat of rust.

The next morning, I helped Steve retrieve a bass lure from the river. Stuck in samsara again? Like bits of magma, my genes had helped form my son, and my habits, dreams, and ignorance had partly shaped him. As a parent, too often I learned things at my children's expense. I was glad Steve asked me to help. In another year he'd be thirteen, a bona fide adolescent, perhaps too ashamed or stubborn to ask again. When sun scattered medallions on the river, I thought, "You're flawed, but not hopeless. Learn from your

57

mistakes." The river might have agreed with Roethke: "We think by feeling. What is there to know?" Think by feeling. The poem, like the river, suggested thinking of a new kind. On the Salmon, I began to feel it.

That same day Suzanne put on her life jacket and paddled an inflated kayak in the shallows. Then she got cocky and headed farther out. The current was stronger than she knew. In a panic, she ditched the kayak and swam hard for shore. Afterwards, ashamed and blue with shock, she skulked to her quarters. Before long everyone in the group had tried to comfort her. Finally, Cheryl coaxed her out for a supper of hash browns and fried bass. Luckily, two rowers managed to retrieve the kayak. That night a crook-necked goose flew honking down the canyon. A comet sailed over rimrock like a molten tear.

Hiking the bench, we found signs of rattler, chukar, and deer. Visitors in a wild place, we made adjustments—slept and ate less, drank more (water, mostly), and let go, or tried to, of everything but where we were. Were we, in fact, more like the river, which, apart from its rapids, flowed calm, deep, and clear? Did we indulge the illusion that we could do without much, if not most, of the industrial civilization that had shaped us? On the porch of an abandoned farmhouse, an old boot scraper made of horseshoes lay intact. Sheila, a loan officer, cracked us up with jokes. Linda, from Seattle, who traveled alone, was on the rebound from a relationship with an older married man who'd been dependent to the point of cruelty. Dan, one of the appraisers, was recently divorced—his wife ran off with a cattle rancher. "At least I have my place to go back to," he quipped. "My new wife is five acres of alfalfa."

58

Before dark, a few of us motored up to China Bar in a small outboard kept at the Hilton. I searched for signs of former inhabitants—lantern fragments, scraps of leather or tin—but souvenir hounds had long since scoured the place. All that remained were chunks of basalt stacked near a lone ponderosa, the crude walls of a pit house Chinese miners had built a century before. Many had suffered at the hands of whites. Far from populous mining camps, the souls at China Bar eked out a life, fishing and hunting like the Nez Perce. Winter in the canyon would be grim. I was thankful for riches of my own—a river and a family to share it with.

China Bar recalled Idaho's rich history. In the lobby of the Clearwater National Forest office in Orofino, there's a piece of driftwood on display. Found on the North Fork of the Clearwater River, it bears a Chinese inscription from 1876, along with a translation, added later:

> *The ninth day of the fifth month*
> *of the third year*
> *of the reign of Kuang Hsii*
> *I have gone into the wilderness*
> *one hundred miles by water*
> *to meet someone.*
> *This stream is half way.*

The text reminded me of a lyric in the *The Book of Songs*, a collection housing intimate moments in the lives of the Chou people of the first millennium B.C. The poems reflect many voices—kings, aristocrats, peasants, soldiers, courtesans, princesses, husbands, wives. For centuries the book served as the basic educational text of the upper classes and for training in diplomacy.

On the bar, I couldn't get *The Book of Songs* out of my head. In China there's a long tradition of learning the poems by heart. The poem I remembered was a love lyric, but I didn't know where the Clearwater version, if it really was one, had come from. Maybe it held a glimpse of turbulent mining years in the American West. Was it addressed from one lover to another? Did the prefect of a district back home come to check up on someone? I'd never know, but for a moment I saw, and felt, deeper into place and time.

⌣

Our last day on the river threatened rain. We'd float Cougar Canyon to the confluence with the Snake, and from there, with the help of an outboard drag on the lead raft, motor twenty miles to the takeout at Heller Bar.

As we approached the mouth of Wapshilli Creek, Steve spotted a large bird about a hundred yards ahead. Perched on the bank, it looked too big to be a hawk. Passing it, we back paddled for a close-up of a mature golden eagle. Imperial but riled, it glared. Then we saw the reason: it stood clutching a fresh-killed fawn. Its mate watched from the opposite bank. We had disturbed a hunting pair about to breakfast. When they spotted our rafts, one must have flown across the river to distract us.

The canyon narrowed and the river gathered speed. It was my turn to ride the inflated kayak. As Dan held it beside the raft, I strapped on a life jacket and helmet, grabbed the paddle, wedged myself into the slot, and slipped into the current. Waves that before had seemed trifling were now huge, but the kayak rode lightly, a bird in rough wind. Instead of smashing into swells, I crested them. When the current slowed, the river seemed bottomless. Columns of refracted light plumbed its tea-colored depth. An arm's reach away, slabs of granite rose knobby and jagged, as if we floated through the rib cage of a prehistoric beast. We glided through rock formations shoved skyward from the basement of the continent. When earth's crust shifted, up they came, like an eruption bubbling through broken skin. Earth too was a beast, breathing and belching in geologic time. The river trembled beneath us.

Great sturgeon live in these waters, most in the Snake. As recently as 1950, fish over twenty feet long, weighing half a ton, have been taken. You fish for them with winches or ocean poles, trawling with a steel leader and bait. One old-timer I knew used a slab of bacon jammed on a fist-sized hook attached to a chain. The greatest sturgeon are gone, but descendents up to twelve feet

60

long still thrive here, protected by a catch-and-release fishery. I conjured armor-plated Leviathans cruising beneath me. Sturgeon are believed to have the lifespan of a human being. In Nez Perce stories they've saved people from drowning. So the river held its mysteries, *pace* St. Augustine: "But you, O Lord...make the deep rivers serve your purposes and govern the raging tide of time."

As I climbed from the kayak back into our raft, light rain fell. The best of the trip was behind us now. Floaters began thinking of their routine lives. We grew more somber and reflective, like the strangers we had been before. As I pilfered our duffel bag for sweatshirts, I wondered about the river. Would it be a stranger to us?

Chad, Sheila's fifteen-year-old, had taken a shine to Suzanne. He fumbled at conversation. When we beached for lunch, he teased her then offered her a cookie. Suzanne was flattered, but polite. When she smiled, I glimpsed the young woman she might become.

Standing on the bank, Steve spotted a large fish grazing. By the time I reached him, it had moved into deeper water. Maybe it was a big smallmouth, a steelhead or rainbow, or some mythological lunker. The water was deep olive, laced with silt. Smaller fish scurried into shadows and the river kept its secrets.

Before we launched again, Cheryl and I stood on the bank hand in hand. The Salmon had revealed part of itself, but as light failed it seemed to withdraw. By late afternoon it was chilly. Wind spit rain in our faces. Cheryl, Steve, and I huddled in slickers. Suzanne wrapped herself in a blanket and closed her eyes. We looked forward to hot baths, snacks, and sleep, and telling Bren, our oldest, who couldn't make the trip because of work, all about it. I would miss the river, and I pledged to come back. As we cinched the rafts onto pickups with bungee cords and rubber grips, I inventoried the loose ends of my life.

On the ride to town, folks were mostly quiet. Some, including our own two, dozed. The appraisers talked about next year's vacation, the boat-people about their next float. In the months ahead we'd remember our time, and no time, in the floating world. I thought of the river's gifts: the tiny figures in Hiroshige's print who walked beside a stream; the slant of sunlight in pools; moss crocheted on rocks beside a spring; the glitter of sand at Dead Man's Creek, and the shade, and white water dashing our faces. I thought of the glare of an eagle's eye, and gestures of kindness, unasked for, that came with our days on the river.

Warmed Twice

When Cheryl said we should get rid of the stove, I balked. She had her reasons. We heated with gas instead of wood now. Our children were grown and gone, and we no longer gathered by a fire. The stove took up space we could use for a stereo, love seat, or chair. She knew I was attached to it and that moving it would be a chore, but she didn't mention her real reason: the thing was an eyesore. The size of a recliner, it was made of rugged quarter-inch steel painted black, with a head plate and skirt, four stubby legs, and a ragged, L-shaped sheet-metal pipe that once drew smoke up the chimney. In a den filled with furniture and potted plants, it was ugly and useless to boot.

For me the stove harbored fire. And fire triggered visions: a man and his son splitting wood on a crisp fall day; flames licking a split larch log on the grate; kids on the sofa munching popcorn and reading stories, with no TV in sight. The fire accompanied us as we launched into "The Little White Duck" with Burl Ives's scratchy tenor crackling on an old 33 rpm while it snowed outside. To Cheryl the stove was in the way. To me it recalled the life of a family. And we were both right.

The thought of moving the stove brought back winters past. When we gathered in the den for snacks or stories, flames would punctuate our chatter. Sap boiled to a hiss and pockets of gas exploded. If I left the stove door slightly ajar, light tangoed on the wall. Wood heat is dry heat. When a fire was burning, the den became a desert. I bought a cast-iron pan, filled it with water, and placed it on the head plate. Now wisps of steam mimicked smoke that rose from the chimney. The stove got hot enough to fry eggs on. When Steve and Suzanne were toddlers, we erected a barricade of chairs for safety. Like the old Roman oven, or *focus*, the stove was the heart of our house and fire was its pulse.

Hearing the fire whetted our appetites, and we wanted to see the flames. I removed the door panel and took it to a window shop where a man cut a piece of tempered glass, fashioned a copper frame, and welded on a handle. The door became a window. I'd catch a child sitting on the floor, mesmerized by the flames. Heat could lull them to sleep. It could also spark visions that reappeared in crayon drawings. If imagination transforms what we see, fire is its living image, a tiger in the forest of the night.

But fire has to be fed and cleaned up after. I'd crumple newspaper and place it on the grate, frame it with kindling, and strike a match. Beneath a roof of split larch, the flames grew. Thoreau wrote, "you can always see a face in the fire," but to do it I had to keep the glass panel clean. After a few fires, it sported a rind of creosote. Each week I'd spray it with oven cleaner, and rub off the grime with newsprint.

Fire can delight, instruct, or terrify. The flames in our stove became Rome burning, a volcano erupting, the leap of a forest fire. We saw the alchemy of carbon born and dying in a moment. In Hindu legend, the destroyer god, Shiva, dances in a halo of flame. *Nirvana* is derived from the image of flame. It means "burnt out" or "ceasing to draw breath": the flame of desire is quenched; the soul released from suffering. In our early life as a family, fire evoked memory and conjured imagination. Sometimes the dead hovered in the taste of soot.

⸪

I first met fire in the house where I grew up. When I couldn't sleep, I'd wander into the hall, and stare through a peephole of our coal furnace. Clinkers glowed at white heat and ashes swirled like comet tails. Coal is fire in stone. Once I knelt in the bin and picked up a chunk of anthracite. It smelled like burnt motor oil, and the smudge took many scrubbings to wash away.

In those days fire was all around us. We lived in Spokane, Washington, during the 1950s, and most nearby towns had sawmills. Each mill had a burner for sawdust and slash, then considered waste wood. Cone-shaped ovens made of scrap metal, they could stand seventy feet high, like huge charred wigwams. Nights from a distance, when flames licked the rivet holes, a burner became a Christmas tree that had swallowed light and was about to explode.

After fishing when my father drove home, sparks rose in flurries and smoke stung my eyes. Once as I lay in the backseat half asleep, the moon rose. When I raised my hand toward the window, my skin glittered. At first, I thought I was dreaming, but fish scales caught the moon's reflection. My fingers winked like mica. As I sat up, we passed a burner whose sparks rose in flurries. Under a sky thick with stars, there was fire. It came out of the night, but also out of me. Flesh, wood, and the dark were beautiful and terrifying. I recalled clinkers in the furnace at home, then clips from the Movietone News came back—fire-bombings of London and Germany and the smoke of Nazi ovens.

Fire was a character in the drama of my childhood. It yawned and spat from the roof of a burning house. It snickered in the fireplace and its smoke stung me to tears. Fire bloomed from the Christ-candle in church on Christmas Eve. It sprang from a match like a flower in a speeded-up film. Fire was the anger in my father's eyes. It was taboo, risk, a wild attraction. When I singed my fingers with a match, the pain was a reckoning. When paper wilted into flakes of ash, I took note. Was this the fate of all things mortal?

⠂⟋

Fire not only warmed us; it linked us to the natural world. Our woodpile held fir and larch I cut in the mountains. Woodcutting became a ritual, and sometimes my oldest son, Bren, went with me. I'd cut wood in June, after snow had melted, before the fire season prevented using a chain saw. We'd cruise logging roads looking for a tree to fell, meet mushroomers after morels and white-tailed deer browsing new grass. Steller's jays set the woods on alert. When one flew, a slice of sky darted through the trees.

Cutting wood was hard work. I'd choose a dead or dying mid-sized fir or larch, with the chain saw make a kerf about three feet up, saw halfway through, then drive in a felling-wedge. A seasoned sawyer would have foregone kerf and wedge on a tree of such modest size, but I was green: I had to be sure which way it would fall. As the saw dug in, whining and spitting, the tree would creak and tremble. Then—*crack, splinter, groan*—it lost its footing, toppled, and crashed to the ground. I trimmed the branches and bucked the trunk into stove lengths. Before long, I was spent. In the lingo of old-timers, I had "made wood."

The chainsaw kept me hopping. I learned how to mix gas and oil, how to lubricate and sharpen the chain, and lug the thirty-pound contraption around. But the thing unnerved me. It was a steel beast with high-speed teeth, ready to throw a tantrum Revved up, it whined like a banshee, and it ate wood at a furious pace. If I hit a knot, the saw could buck violently, and if the bar got pinched, the chain would bind.

At times I was prisoner to a machine. Once on a steep slope, a standing snag pinched the bar so the chain got stuck. As I struggled to free it, the snag snapped off, and I leapt from its path just in time. The saw leapt with me, teeth whirring once more, just missing my arm. Blood caught my throat, but it was fear I tasted. I realized working alone was lunacy, and chose not to cut on steep ground again. One slip and I'd have bled to death before I made it to the truck. Later, it dawned on me: a tool enforces natural limits, but a machine has a life of its own. In a few days, one man with a chain saw can topple a small forest.

But I wanted to know fire. Cutting wood I felt I'd earned the right. And there were bonuses. Once I forgot to retrieve the axe. A week later, I found it leaning against the stump where I'd left it. Nearby, in the duff, a mushroom had sprouted—a stinkhorn stretching for sun. Rudely phallic, it stood proud. Yellow ooze

66

dribbling from its cap left a faint stench in the air. The fecundity of the woods heartened me. In the topsoil new life smoldered. Dew steamed like smoke, lilies unfolded, and shoots of new grass appeared. Wood from the forest had warmed our home, but now the earth itself heated up. Other lives were waking—paintbrush and lupine, gnat and swallowtail, and the brash, unsavory stinkhorn—all warmed to the planet's inner fire.

My work followed a seasonal rhythm. I'd cut wood in the spring and split it in the fall. I rediscovered what I'd known as a boy working in the potato fields and as a carpenter's assistant—the rhythm of bodily labor. I sweated for the fires to come. The axe recalled why chain gangs work to song. If I forced a stroke, wood thwarted the blade. I'd pause, take a breath, relax, and start over. Soon the axe was an extension of my arm, its stroke a rough music.

To cut wood well, follow the grain. Growth rings in a log are pathways, like the Tao, the "way" of things. You can go with them and proceed, or against them and hack on into futility. Writing demands similar patience and precision. Words track invisible meaning. But in life, as in writing, sometimes it's better to shut up. When I coached Bren through his axe stroke, we both got irked. By suggesting a "right way," I upset his rhythm, or his attempt to find it. Rules were not the Tao. When I went back to work, he got the hang of splitting wood on his own. On good days our work seemed effortless. The *tunk* of an axe was its measure, a drum sounding an overture to winter.

⁓

A forest holds subterranean fire. The dead feed the living and the living feed each other in a dance of biomass at work. Windfall rots to become rich turf, and the term dead wood finds new meaning. The forest is a living laboratory. Once we found cedar saplings sprouted from a rotting parent log. They grew in a row, straight as the trunk that fed them, faithful to the spirit of their elder, whose ruin shot them skyward, though the family was too large to stay healthy. Exposed on a cut bank, fungi clamped on fir roots grew in ritual symbiosis. The feast radiates out, down and in. A tree feeds air with carbon dioxide, feeds us with fire, and fungi feed mice, shrews, or voles, which in turn feed owls, foxes, or coyotes. The web widens. I wanted to burn wood so I could come back and cut more. The journey—of seed to sprout to cone to wood to flame—helped make me whole. I was an agent of real estate that would burn, an instrument of fire who brought the forest into our home as light.

Our woodpile harbored other worlds. Each fall I covered it with a tarp to keep it dry and over the winter neighbors moved in. Crickets, ants, beetles, and spiders nested in bark cracks. Night crawlers squeezed under damp wood and moths hatched from cocoons wedged in pecker holes. Wood held doors and windows. A split log revealed cricket caves, ant roads, and the whorls of knots. Our cat used the woodpile as a scratching station and left her glyphs in the bark. Termites and carpenter ants gnawed pith to a spongy dust and on the inner bark beetles carved a labyrinth of paths, like designs from Celtic art. Larch bark is a crazy quilt of flaky orange layers, thick and scab-like. It looks like a jigsaw puzzle or a topographic map of rugged terrain and smells like turpentine. Pitch is the forest's perfume. Writing too recalls the pathways of wood. Originally *write* meant "to carve." Scribble in a field book and you score the flesh of trees.

◦

Each fall, I faced the regimen of chimney cleaning: screw together fiberglass rods with threaded ends to form a long, pliant pole; tie on a square wire brush; attach an iron weight from my son's gym set; lug the wobbly contraption up a ladder, place it on the roof, then haul myself up. Straddling the roof crown, fighting vertigo, I raised the pole over the chimney hole and lowered the brush into the blackness. When it dead-ended, I jerked the pole like a pump handle to scrape creosote from the chimney walls. A flash fire could spit cinders onto our cedar shake roof and trigger Armageddon. Cheryl knew it and I honored her fear. As I yanked on the pole, creosote silted the autumn air.

Cultures and subcultures can be fire-specific. Hawaiians honor volcanic eruptions spewing magma and ash. In Ohio and Pennsylvania, steelworkers feed blast furnaces that roar like the devil, while vats pour molten ore into trays in a version of hell's factories. In the Northwest, smoke jumpers risk their lives parachuting into backcountry to dash spot fires or fight full-blown conflagrations. Near large cities, nuclear reactors etch the skyline, and people pass them uneasily, sensing what's inside. In South American rain forests, as land is burned for farming or grazing, smoke shrouds the sun. The flames raise dark omens. Developers destroy plants and animals that might bring cures for cancer, AIDS, or plagues as yet unknown. If I could choose a role, I'd be a Native American fire keeper, who chooses rocks for the sweat-lodge fire. He or she must choose carefully. Heat releases not only sweat and impurities, but also the wisdom of earth, stone, and flame.

I think back to the original fire—before the woodstove and the furnace of my childhood. Back so far I no longer think, but envision. I'm a boy led with others into a cave deep underground. Except for the torch ahead of us, it's pitch dark. Then the torch goes out. Blackness swallows us. We're lost in the abyss of absolute silence.

When the torch is rekindled, light dances on the walls of a vast cavern. We're in the womb of a beast that has swallowed light. Then pieces of light start taking shape. A saber-toothed tiger flashes awake in the stone. A herd of bison stampedes across the wall. Antelope and deer roam, hunters with spears and bows, and figures part human, part beast. In the dark, I witness the hunt that occurs above me, in the country of light. Thanks to fire, I discover who I am. Cave paintings tell a story fire lets me read. I'm attracted not only to animals and stone, but to flames that quicken them.

69

When Steve, our youngest, turned seven, I'd find burnt matchsticks under his bed. I warned him about the danger, but for six months he couldn't help it. Fire mesmerized him. He flirted with the kiss of a spark, when phosphorous leapt to flame. He honored fire's candor and savored its risk. Matches held hidden power and like a would-be Prometheus he conjured it. One afternoon he and a neighbor boy hauled scrap lumber to an old overturned boxcar in the field next to us. The fire got so big it scared them silly. We unrolled our longest hose and managed to douse the flames. Steve's eyes said I didn't have to scold him.

·‿

My father wants to be cremated when he dies. He was a shrewd businessman, and in death he'll follow suit—be tidy, efficient, not buy a casket or plot. He told me I could spread his ashes on my mother's grave or in the Idaho lake he loved.

How we view the dead depends on how we see the living. Mummification assumes the body and soul are inseparable. Christian burial looks to the resurrection of the body, the flesh incorruptible. In India, a corpse burned beside the Ganges becomes ash on sacred water, and the soul returns to Brahma. Some Native American tribes raised the dead on scaffolds where, through the work of birds and insects, they returned to air as spirit.

My father's decision suits him, and I may choose it for myself. Fire will lick me clean. If bonemeal can make fertilizer, I may be useful. A sealed coffin only holds an idea of life, and a strange one at that—as if we could preserve the body in some permanent way, as if we'd want to. I'd choose a plywood box soon to rot, become worm fuel or fish food cast on the water. After death, my burnt calcium will lend its ounce to loam. I won't burn in hell, but smolder in the heaven I know.

When my mother died, none of us saw beyond a conventional burial. But now I think she'd have preferred fire. It would have matched the cancer that consumed her. Recently, visiting her

70

grave, I remembered our church pastor, a stocky, balding Scotsman named Redfield, who gave impassioned sermons. My mother called him fiery. At first I thought she meant his complexion, which had a bright reddish tint (I later learned he suffered from acne rosacea). But she probably meant his voice. The lyrical force he gave to the Psalms, read from the King James Version, reminded her of fire.

Language is a fire that can warm and illuminate, or else anger and consume. When the spirit descended at Pentecost, the disciples spoke with tongues of flame. The apostle James wrote, "And the tongue is a fire...With it we bless the Lord and Father, and with it we curse men who are made in the likeness of God." James knew that words demand responsibility; they can heal or destroy. When I told Bren how to split wood, he grew impatient, but when I was quiet and taught by example, he found his way. My mother wrote colorful letters and with practice might have been a poet, fiery with words. Emily Dickinson compared the soul to the "white heat" of ore that quivers from the forge and burns with "unanointed blaze."

·→

But the stove had to go. We no longer needed wood heat; wood smoke poisoned the valley's air; and forests where I cut wood had been badly overlogged. I gave my chain saw to my son, Bren, and sold my wood-hauling trailer to a neighbor. Now it was time to part with the stove.

Home from college, Steve, the one-time match lover, volunteered to help. We put newspapers on the concrete slab where the stove stood. When I loosened the pipe, soot fell like inky snow. We were closing a chapter in the history of a family. After removing the pipe and gathering soot, we edged the stove off the slab and jockeyed it through the back door. In its temporary home on the patio, it looked desolate, its life gone up in smoke. What before had seemed almost alive was now an empty wreck, just steel, bolts, and paint. As we hauled it through the door, I felt

71

the stirrings of this essay. Like Thoreau, who dug stumps from his bean field and later split them to burn, I was warmed twice.

On a bright June morning, we hoisted the stove into the pickup. The frame was cold—the stove had been out all night. As we wrestled with it, I shivered. Skidding, shoving, tipping, and hoisting, we worked up a sweat. Finally we got the cumbersome thing onto the truck. On the drive to the recycling yard, I glanced into the rearview mirror. The hole for the stovepipe gaped. The stove not only looked out of place, but betrayed—a bulky, decapitated hulk emptied of light and hope. What defied logic, lived in my imagination. I could distinguish fire from steel, but not separate them.

When I drove onto the weigh-scale and stopped, the woman at the window waved me back. Somehow, I had triggered the alarm. The scale's electronic sensors picked up radioactivity. When I pulled off and drove on a second time, no bell sounded. The alarm signaled dislocation, a rent in time. My cargo wasn't scrap metal, but a keeper of fire—the focus that had kept a family warm.

I drove into the scrap yard, past mounds of junked iron and steel—oil drums, the driving wheels and rails of trains, cracked girders, housings of table saws and lathes, stacks of rebar, steel poles, hubcaps, and buckets—all the molded metal imaginable dumped in a mountainous graveyard by the tracks. A young man wearing overalls and heavy boots sat in his car eating a sandwich. When he saw me, he got out and pointed to a dumping spot. "Nice stove," he said as he helped me wrestle it from the truck. I nodded in silence. Just then the recycling yard was still. The driver of a top loader was also on his lunch break. The stove toppled from the tailgate, landed with a thud in the dirt, and tipped onto its side. The door flung open and coughed a mouthful of soot on the ground. As I turned to go, bits of it hung like smoke in the heavy summer air.

The Patience of Hawks

On a windy morning in April, I sat at the kitchen table scribbling on a notepad. Friends had asked Cheryl and me to lead a writing workshop, and we'd been brainstorming. As I gathered stray thoughts, she took a break to do chores. When I glanced out at the walnut tree, a large hawk had perched midway up. It clutched a limb, bobbing in the stiff gusts. The hawk might have spotted finches at the feeder a few feet below and landed in hopes of getting breakfast.

As I stared the muscles in my neck tightened, as if *I* were prey. The hawk's gaze was riveting, a powerful, no-nonsense ferocity, as intense as it was direct. When the raptor arrived, the finches must have fled, for it owned the walnut now. It glanced eagerly about, ready to strike if a meal got close enough.

Hawks frequent these parts—in river canyons, patches of forest, and edges of wheat fields. Redtails scout from power pole lookouts, preying on voles or mice. They're buzzard hawks, or *Buteos*, the robust-bodied, short-tailed birds we see soaring over a field or prairie. *Accipiters* (Latin for "hawk," literally "taker," "voracious one") are bird hawks, smaller-bodied, long-tailed forest dwellers. They include Swainson's, Sharp-shinned, and Cooper's, and prey on smaller birds. Ospreys patrol the river corridors and peregrines the far breaks. In our rural suburb, kestrels hover copter-like to ambush smaller birds or insects. There are two redtail nests near the road I take to work—one on a canyon ledge, the other high in a cottonwood. This spring, inspecting the ledge nest with field glasses, I spotted a pair of fledglings. They were the size of adult pigeons, white and wooly-headed, peering over thatch at the world.

The hawk in our tree was the largest I've been close to—from tail tip to crown it looked well over two feet in height. It performed an awkward jig, tucking first one foot, then another, under a wing.

Hawk in the hay—UP—hawk in the straw—DOWN (repeat with other foot). Maybe it jockeyed for balance, got a leg up on warmth, or hid its orange talons a set at a time, for camouflage. Maybe it performed calisthenics of a sort unmentioned in field guides. Whatever the case, its behavior made me more aware of my own.

The hawk perched just a few yards beyond our sliding glass door. To say I was curious would be misleading: I had an almost predatory urge to see. My feelings lurched one way, my thoughts another. I feared the hawk would fly before I got a good look. A gift had dropped into our backyard. What would receiving it ask of me?

The hawk was too big to be a kestrel, Sharp-shinned, or Swainson's. It probably wasn't a buzzard hawk—they prefer small mammals as prey. Not wanting to startle the raptor, I got up slowly and retrieved binoculars and a field guide. I honed in on details. The hawk had a buff breast with dark brown streaks, a superciliary line or "eyebrow", and a dark, flared crown and rounded tail with white terminal band. Its cere, a small patch of skin above the upper mandibles, was a bright yellow-orange, its talons true orange, and the pupils and beak tip jet black. These features were distinctive of a Cooper's, and I prided myself, thinking I'd guessed right.

But what did such identifiers tell me? Descriptors in the field guide ("crown is darker than nape; underparts appear rufous") were clinical and detached, but here was a living, breathing raptor on the alert. Trying to identify surface features was engaging, but I wanted to know more. After close scrutiny, Cooper's still seemed right—but by then seeing wasn't just technical. I had to—needed to—let the hawk have its way with me.

If I thought too much, the Cooper's became an abstraction. I tried sketching it, but wind jostled its perch. I squinted through field glasses until my eyes ached, but the hawk wouldn't let me settle. It gazed intensely (everywhere at once, it seemed) and set me on edge. I was far from what Buddhists call "awareness without grasping," but at times, seeing was everything. The hawk and I were one, or so I felt—before thought. When the feeling left, I marveled at the hawk's staying power and doubted my own. This hawk was teaching me how to see. If it took a meal, I wanted to be watching.

⤳

With a real predator on hand, plans for a writing workshop seemed beside the point. What was a writing-prompt when a hawk was staring you in the face? I was hardly a naturalist. I recalled John Baker, who, after years of observing peregrines, called himself a "hawk hunter." His advice to beginners? Stay alert, take a bird on its own terms, in its own place, and cultivate the wisdom the body knows. Hawk hunter. I hoped someday to earn the title. The Cooper's seemed a promising, if awkward, start.

Looking back, I see how fickle I was. At first I sentimentalized the event. Here came the hawk, and here sat the watcher, a Thoreau wannabe. I easily succumbed to distraction. In my rush for artificial aids—field glasses, field guides, camera, pen, notebook—I ignored a crucial necessity: bare attention. It was only later, after the hawk had gone, that I recalled the importance, and the challenge, of seeing clearly, without attachment. But at the time clarity was fleeting. Often I floundered.

The longer the hawk stayed put, the more attached I got. In uncanny moments, the hawk seemed to rub off on me. As Baker notes, "the hunter becomes what he hunts." But I didn't kid myself: there was a gulf between the hawk and me. It grew in proportion to the fierceness in the bird's eyes and the flickering uncertainty in my own. There was no self-awareness in the Cooper's gaze, only readiness, sharp as a talon or beak.

⤳

As I kid, I ignored birds for the most part. Once, trying out a friend's new air rifle, I took aim at a sparrow perched in a nearby pine. I

75

trained the crosshairs on its tiny breast and squeezed the trigger. It was as if a miniature balloon suddenly deflated and dropped to my feet. Soft and warm, the sparrow seemed asleep, but its neck went limp in my hands. As I held the poor thing, my gut festered. Even now, a sparrow's ghost lands on my shoulder to scold me.

When I was ten, I met an owl in the woods. A juvenile snowy, it was asleep on the branch of a pine an arm's reach away. We faced each other at eye level. Then it opened its eyes, turned its head full circle, and became a cloud with a face. Did it sense the presence of another living being, one with the same habit of staring? The owl looked into and through me, as if I weren't there, yet somehow we were kin. Call it a child's projection, but the snowy struck a nerve. Maybe it was my totem; maybe it got me ready for the hawk.

‧⁀

Watching the Cooper's I could concentrate for only so long. I'd make a cup of tea, scribble a note to myself, or feel guilty for not helping Cheryl with chores. The hawk's attention seemed far keener than my own. I doubted the wisdom of staring, but the hawk wouldn't let go of me. As for staying power, it won hands down. As I thought of making another cup of tea, from nowhere, a finch appeared. It darted from a nearby pine to the feeder and back, pecking seed then taking cover, apparently oblivious to the predator a few feet away.

At first the hawk didn't seem to notice. It stayed in its perch, jockeying for balance in the wind. But when the Cooper's looked down, its glare seemed to magnify and telescope at the same time. The air went dense, as if flexed by an exchange of ions, and the hair on my neck bristled. The hawk leaned to one side, as if it were dozing, then simply toppled from the limb of the tree. It defied descriptions in the field guide, according to which *Accipiters* are "reckless in the pursuit of prey." The Cooper's seemed cautious, even deliberate. Branches, foliage, and the risk of alerting the

76

finch meant the hawk couldn't dive freely. Instead, it simply "fell" a few feet, and spreading its wings in a momentary hover, lunged. Did the situation trigger noninstinctive behavior in the hawk, a nano-second of thought?

The attack ended as quickly as it began. The finch was too quick for the Cooper's—it made a smart U-turn and fled to a nearby pine. "The hawk went after a finch, but missed!" I hollered at Cheryl. "No kidding!" she yelled from the bathroom upstairs. Things settled down after that. The hawk flew back to its perch. It would have to wait longer and so would I.

◦

I had watched the hawk for about three hours when Cheryl peered into the kitchen. "Remember shopping? The health club? Still wanna go? . . . *Bill*," she urged. I glanced up and she repeated herself. "Sorry," I mumbled, "I'll get my gear." Stuffing my sweats into a duffel bag, I was grateful that the hawk had come. But I had promises to keep. "Count yourself lucky," I thought. "Three hours were more than you could have hoped for."

Before we left the house, the hawk left its perch again. It rose, circled the yard, and landed in the cherry about ten yards from the walnut. I dropped my duffel bag and picked up the field glasses. The Cooper's was easier to see now. Its breast was light buff, with streaks tawny as deer hide, and its talons were the orange of duck feet. In the cherry it seemed even more alert. It danced no jig, but held the limb tightly, its talons like vice grips.

As we pulled out of the driveway, the hawk flew again. The sound of our engine may have startled it. This time, it landed in a small apple tree near the back fence. Cheryl granted me a last look. While she waited in the car, I hurried back into the house and picked up the glasses. In its new perch, the hawk's camouflage was exquisite. Branches of the apple (in need of pruning) were gray and crosshatched, their buds just breaking into tiny splashes of white. The hawk's body nestled in the arc of the limbs, as if a

77

dark urn rested there. When we finally left, the day was poised for an ambush once more.

The hawk offered an extended lesson in seeing. Sometimes I could stare and still be aware of myself. Restlessness eased and I floated in repose, as if the hawk and I dreamed each other. I thought of the advice of the Zen priest, Shunryu Suzuki: "if you fix your mind on the activity with some confidence, the quality of your state of mind is that activity itself." For a moment, Buddhist logic unnerved me. Were there times when the quality of my mind *was* the hawk? For the Cooper's the quality of mind was seeing, an ocular ferocity driven by genes and blood. As Baker writes, "the eye becomes insatiable for hawks." He refers to the eye of the hawk hunter, but by implication also the hawk's eye. If you suspend the filtering reason and focus on bodily attention, you attend to the other directly. You open to reflect it, and it reflects you. As far as imagination and sensory faculties allow, you *become* it. Maybe it actually happened—I had no way of knowing. Was I like Keats at his window, watching a sparrow? "I take part in its existence and pick about the gravel." I don't think the hawk ever saw me. How could it have known what it was looking at? But I felt the shock of being in its eye. The Cooper's was a measure of my ability, and inability, to see.

·ﾉ

On our way to the health club, we stopped at a book and video store. While Cheryl browsed the movie racks, I perused the book section. I looked over a few field guides, then found an oversized book entitled *Birds*. It was a collection of paintings by the Canadian artist, Robert Bateman, known for his depictions of wildlife. The portraits were sharply imagined and celebrated birds in their natural habitats. A painting of a red-tailed hawk took me to the snow-swept prairie where Bateman found it. Later, as an experiment, I tried to put the painting into words. The boundary between language and image quickly exerted itself. Saying too much clouded what I saw, and saying too little diminished it. Where was that fine line? Could it ever be crossed?

From the ruins of a fallen tree, a snag juts into winter sky. In the foreground, the trunk catches your eye, dead wood plastered with snow. Gray, spindly, and half stripped of bark, the snag climbs from left to right. Near the tip, its back toward you, a hawk has perched. The sky wears a winter blanket of gray, and the hawk and tree trunk are a rich brown. These darker colors highlight snowflakes biting the air. Seen from behind, its feathers like a tapered skirt, the hawk turns its head your way and so, in effect, sees you. Only one eye is visible, an amber oval pierced by a bead of ebony. The hawk's beak curves down toward the trunk, and its tail feathers, twin struts of russet, point straight down, matching the dead wood. The parallel suggests camouflage and is pleasing to the eye. Alert, yet in repose, fierce against the cold, the hawk is a bundle of umber life. The more you look, the more parts of the scene converge, snow dots connecting stump, hawk, and sky, like pointillist hail.

Admiring Bateman's birds, I thought of Audubon. The portraits in *Birds of America* are meticulously detailed, painted in watercolor with almost photographic precision, in a prephotographic age. Typically, an Audubon bird is viewed on or near the tree or bush it nests in, feeds on, or both. The approach is scientific, focusing on the bird itself, as an empirical object, apart from, or highlighted by, its surroundings. That may be why Audubon's birds are so often chosen for logos, book covers, or emblems—they're simple, direct, pleasant to look at, and stand apart, often in dramatic poses.

Bateman's presentation is different. His approach might be termed "ecological." His birds are vividly, yet intimately, part of a place, as if you'd stepped into their territory unawares. The difference between the two painters no doubt reflects taste and temperament, but also the spirit of two ages—the objectivity of enlightenment rationalism versus the mutuality of contemporary ecology.

79

Something about Audubon's portraits had always troubled me, but until I saw Bateman's work, I couldn't put my finger on it. Audubon observed birds closely and painted them in dramatic poses, with accuracy, elegance, and a sense of color unequaled in his time. But somehow, despite this, his birds often look frozen. His approach may have lent itself to this. Typically, he trapped or shot a bird he wanted to paint; gutted and preserved it; then posed it on wires in his studio. He wanted to get the subject right, but in doing so he risked turning it into an object, apart from its surroundings. Clearly, Audubon wished to imply the illusion of an actual landscape, but by focusing on the bird apart, he produced a still life. You get an accurate, detailed portrait of a creature frozen in time.

Bateman's approach turns on mutuality. He brings us into the habitat of the animal or bird in question. His paintings are detailed too. With help from photographs and field notes, they attend carefully to a given place. Seeing his work, we may choose to be analytical, as with Audubon. But we're also welcomed into a habitable place on earth, one we momentarily share with a creature who belongs there.

Looking at Bateman's work and recalling the Cooper's, I sensed radical disparities. There's a difference between careful, detached observing and impassioned seeing. A great painter practices both. In his own way each of these artists bore witness to a life beyond our control. Audubon may have wanted to, or felt he could, control it; Bateman sought to evoke or reveal it. As I pondered the difference, I realized what the Cooper's was teaching me.

In the pool at the health club a man was paddling on a float tube. Bald, a fringe of white on his temples, he looked well into his seventies. I was doing my labored crawl in the lane next to him. Stopping to catch our breaths, we nodded but didn't speak. He seemed kind and pleased with his exercise. If I was middle-aged, he was elderly, but we were kin. He swam with ease and grace. No diehard, he enjoyed his bodily life. I thought of the hawk paddling through high air. Had it made a kill and resumed its journey? Like this aging swimmer, the Cooper's held a capacity for grace. In a world both beautiful and precarious, it marked our mortal promise. For that I owed it greater respect.

When Cheryl and I got home, the hawk was nowhere in sight. I went into the kitchen to make tea and glanced into the yard. In the wake of the raptor's departure, all was still. There were no birds at the feeder now. But something wasn't right. It dawned on me gradually. The scene was familiar—the lawn, the walnut and cherry, and beyond them the garden and fence. But a hitch in vision drew my attention to a far corner of the yard. Something wanted to come into focus. A fence post near the apple tree had grown taller. It had grown an appendage, and suddenly that appendage was the hawk. The Cooper's had stayed after all, only now it wasn't waiting. Perched on the post, it clutched something, pecked hard, tore off a strip of flesh and bolted it down. Field glasses showed its talons pierced a bloody lump. The few remaining feathers looked like a robin's.

After the hawk left for good, it often visited my thoughts. It would surface at odd times—when I was drying dishes or on my way to work. When I thought of it flying, its wing beats took the rhythm of my pulse. Sometimes the rhythm slowed; sometimes it speeded up. I had the sense, however strange, that the Cooper's wanted to tell me something. I stopped to watch hawks more often after that. At times I sensed their unseen presence and felt like prey.

John Baker points out that the foveal cells in a peregrine's retina afford a resolution eight times greater than our own. With both lateral and binocular vision, a hawk picks up a moving object in the land or air below it. Like a hunter's high-powered scope, its eyes bring the prey into focus. It's as if the target gets larger as you aim. Imagine squatting on a power pole to glimpse a mouse in the stubble below. Now imagine doing it from a half-mile up. When a hawk zeroes in on it, a mouse or finch is the center of the universe. Often dead center.

Once I stopped by a wheat field to watch a redtail perched on a power pole. It swooped down, glided in a low arc, snatched a rodent from a furrow and hauled it back to the pole. The approach was savage, elegant, beautiful, and precise. The hawk descended slowly and just before it would have touched the ground, hovered for a second, struck, then rose, clutching its prey. Its focus was flawless. The approach, strike, and retrieval were choreographed, like a dance, somnambulant at first, then ferocious. In a flash the top of the pole snapped off, sprouted wings, swooped to the ground then rose and reattached itself, all effortlessly, with poise, strength, and grace.

·

As I watched the Cooper's gobble robin, I too was fed. I witnessed the upshot of the hawk's cunning and skill, but also its patience. Call it instinct, if you like, but how is that different from human will, the discipline of waiting? Patience is a trait we share with some animals or birds. As we grieve are we different from the elephant who revisits the body and bones of its kin for days, sniffing them, rubbing them with its trunk, nodding and swaying its great head in what must be one of the most moving images of loss we can witness? *Patience* is from the Latin *patior*, "to suffer or endure." I recalled my own patience, and impatience, watching the hawk. The Cooper's taught me something about endurance, the willingness to suffer for what you need or admire, or in the case of a hawk with young, for what others need too.

82

Maybe any attempt to navigate the gulf between species is mere wish-fulfillment or futile speculation, beneath the purview of hard science. But recalling the Cooper's, I take heart. Reason tells me it never sensed my presence, but imagination feeds that promise. Who's to say? Maybe we shared a mutual patience, a respect—"re-seeing"—born of the eye. Maybe we were hooked on looking, the hawk for a meal and I for more ethereal, but no less sustaining, food.

.

When the Cooper's left for good, I walked out to see where it had taken its meal. The post held a smear of blood, and a few small feathers lay on the lawn. The hawk had gorged on the robin. It consumed nearly everything—feathers, flesh, ribs, skull, internal organs—all but a pair of helpless claws that lay on the grass. Later, behind a row of pines, I found a second pair of claws. The hawk had taken two robins in one day. I reviewed the kills in my mind's eye—how the Cooper's lunged from its hideout, clutched a bird, and crushed its neck. Kill, eat, be eaten; live to go on, or die. Woven into this elementary rhythm is a kind of waiting. Call it compassion—a creature suffers to feed itself and its kind. I lifted a feather from the lawn. It was the wrong color for a robin's. A hawk feather perhaps. I took it inside up to my study and wedged it between two books on the shelf, like a flag, beneath a picture of our children.

Hiking the Selway at Night

I woke shivering, my sleeping bag no match for September in the Bitterroots. In the Selway River canyon, pines bristled with frost. Stiff and groggy in the bed of my truck, I poked my head from the bag then quickly dove back in. But it was no use. If I didn't move, and soon, I'd be hypothermic, and that would be that. I rose, stretched, pulled on my boots, chomped a granola bar, and stamped around the truck slugging myself. I had to get warm enough to hike. My watch read three a.m. Hours ago, as I dozed, an owl called in the woods. Now, its half-remembered echo was an alarm whose batteries were failing.

The sky was blackish purple, scatter-gunned with stars. To the east Venus hung like a pendant, but stargazing only made me shiver. My plan was to camp at the trailhead, hike upriver, and spend the day fishing back, but I hadn't counted on a night of hard cold.

Instead of letting the truck heater thaw me out, I chose to hit the trail. I wrestled on my fishing vest, stuffed a day pack with bottled water and snacks, snapped my fly rod together, switched on my penlight, locked the truck and trudged past a marker, *Selway River Trail*. I didn't sign the register—I'd be back by nightfall. My light carved a tiny oval out of darkness.

The trail was rocky and rootbound and I moved warily. The woods were so still the least sound seemed to ricochet. A twig snapped like a gunshot. I was alert now, my senses like trip wires. In spite of the cold, odors laced the air—dry weeds, cottonwood, willow. Then silence turned into sound. Somewhere to my right, a rushing noise grew louder. Unseen, the river moved like wind. But there was something else, a deeper, intermittent downbeat, that mingled with, then countered, my pulse. Swept downstream by the current, stones trundled along, thunking the river's dream work.

The penlight worked well, and then, as if to complete the thought, it flickered and went out. "Shit," I blurted. Hadn't I replaced the batteries just days before? I had been walking only half an hour. I fumbled with the switch, but it was no use. Held just inches from my eyes, my hand was a scrap of pale cloth.

I slipped off my pack, propped my fly rod on a ghostly bush, and sat on a bank near the trail. I remembered hiking here with my children, but the images faded and others rose—a bear foraging, a cougar prowling. I crossed my legs and began deep breathing. Thoughts came and went. I tried not to cling to them, then tried not to try. I breathed slowly, part of the cold and dark.

᳁

A clear May morning on the upper Selway. Bren, just ten, spots a merganser hen with young paddling downstream. "Dad, are they ducks?" he asks. He is lithe and supple, his hair like flax in the sun.

> *On the far bank, a boy stands waving.*
> *Through night-vapor ducks puddle away.*

Now Bren spots three otters swimming upstream. One somersaults into a backstroke and throws us a quizzical look. It says we're strangers here. We may visit, but we don't belong. After a fitful night in the tent, we're worn out, but dawn is bracing. Sun sweeps fog off the river. Dried grass is sweated with smoke. Before we hike out, Bren stuffs half an elk rack into his pack.

᳁

Had minutes passed? Hours? In the darkness vague shapes appeared: there a log, there a blind of branches. Held close, my fingers looked like stubs of wax. Bushes loomed, or was it fog? Were those lumps in the path boulders? Was that, in fact, the path? I saw no stars. Maybe mist hid them or the trees were too thick. From the far bank, a shaft of light leaned down. I inventoried possibilities: a stray moon ray; the first crease of dawn; or, absurdly, the tractor-beam of a UFO. But there was no moon, dawn was at least two hours off, and aliens—well, I was the one who best fit that category. The "beam" just hung there, dim and elongated, hard to distinguish from the darkness.

Night still ruled. I tried to temper my eagerness for dawn. The next time I glanced up, I *saw* what I'd been looking at. It was the trunk of a dead tree leaning from the *near* bank outward. Old and bleached, it looked like the beam of a flashlight in fog. Maybe my eyes had adjusted or dawn had come. The snag looked bodiless, a shaft of light hung in a vacuum of darkness.

In its general diffusion, river sound had tricked me. What had been a dislocated rushing noise now appeared dimly about ten yards to my right, as if thousands of ermine ran on a treadmill. It was still too dark to hike safely, but the half-hour walk and deep breathing had warmed me.

·ᵘ

August on the Selway. Suzanne, now twelve, clutches my shirttail. A moment ago we surprised a baby rattler sunning near the trail. She scolds me about it, and I try to humor her. As we hurry on, the rattler's chirr of warning dims behind us, bearings of an old lawn mower run downhill.

I'm glad for the Selway rattler. I want Suzanne to see what's here, get to know her neighbors. I want to comfort her, too, but just now her adrenaline's in charge.

"We have to keep moving, Dad."

"I know, kiddo. I'll watch for snakes."

For now she needs indulgence, not a lecture. We shuffle along in a clumsy train, I the engine, she the caboose.

> *The river winks brilliantly, day-stars in an emerald sky.*
> *A pine fire hosts the punk of needles.*

·ᵘ

Pieced through trees, the sky was a velvet pincushion, but it was still too dark to walk safely. The woods recalled former visitors. A few years earlier, when a friend hiked the Selway trail near Moose Creek Ranger Station, a man bounded from the brush. He wore only a loincloth, carried a hunting bow, and said he was having a "wilderness experience" and that clothing or gear would spoil it. I thought of shady characters like Bill Moreland, the "ridge runner," who during the forties and fifties lived here as a vagabond and fugitive, stealing food from campers and ranchers then fleeing into the wilderness.

And there were ghosts. In June of 1979 a photographer from the *Spokesman Review* was hiking with a friend below the Selway Lodge, a private holding in the heart of the wilderness. Suddenly a plane roared over and to the horror of the men dropped one of its engines. The photographer got a shot of the flaming engine as it fell. A moment later, the second engine feathered out, and the DC-3 lurched into a crash dive. It came in low, snapped off the crown of a tall tree, flipped, and plunged into the river at Wolf Creek Rapid, killing twelve of the fourteen Forest Service workers aboard. The grim business of salvaging the wreck went on for days.

The year after we arrived in Idaho, two members of a Selway float party drowned when their raft overturned in rapids. Like the rugged country it drained, the river could be treacherous.

> *Close your eyes.*
> *Fragments of burning metal shear through pines.*
> *In the river a current of blood dissolves.*

From Hidden Lake in North Central Idaho's Bitterroot range, 87 the headwaters of the Selway gather to creek-sized strength, tumbling some twenty-five miles to Magruder Guard Station on the Nez Perce Trail Road. This rugged, seasonal road forms a boundary between the River of No Return Wilderness and the Selway-Bitterroot Wilderness, combined areas the size of New

Hampshire. From Magruder the Selway flows north, meandering through canyons toward the mouth of Moose Creek. There, cutting beneath a patchwork of granite peaks, ridges, saddles, and high lakes carved into the western slope of the Idaho Rockies, it swings west and runs another twenty-five miles to Selway Falls.

As a designated Wild and Scenic River, Idaho's upper and middle Selway are protected from development. Provisions of the Wilderness Act of 1964 keep its watershed from being roaded, mined, or logged. The lower roaded stretch, where I often camped with my family, is noted for calm, clear pools and tranquil current. Though its origin is uncertain, *Sal-wah* may combine Nez Perce and Shoshone words meaning, roughly, "good canoe water" or "sound of water flowing."

In the dark those quiet lower stretches seemed far away. Slowly the map in my head dissolved. Cold stung my cheeks. Damp mops of grass soaked up river-sound. I wanted to hit the trail, embrace what would come, which just then wasn't daylight, but dark.

Or was it? Were those surreal lumps I thought could be boulders actual boulders now? I got up, stretched, yawned. I could see just enough to hobble slowly along. A year later, reading Peter Matthiessen's *The Snow Leopard*, an account of his six-month trek through high ranges of Tibet and Nepal, I would relive my night on the river. Matthiessen recalls advice from an expert on Tantric meditation-walking:

> *The walker must neither speak, nor look from side to side. He must keep his eyes fixed on a single distant object and never allow his attention to be attracted by anything else. When the trance has been reached, though normal consciousness is for the greater part suppressed, it remains sufficiently alive to keep the man aware of the obstacles in his way, and mindful of his direction and goal.*

Matthiessen met several of these walkers. They negotiated steep trails in high mountain passes, and there are well-authenticated accounts of their being able to walk this way in the dark. Though

I had practiced Zen, I thought better of walking "blind." I was a beginner with small confidence in second sight. Matthiessen made me wonder how far meditative practice could take me. Surely, the Buddhists are right: much of our thinking only gets in the way. With practice, emptiness would calm us, but too often we're bogged with clutter. If I could suspend thinking, trust intuition, and practice focused breathing . . .

Beyond knifelike outlines of trees, patches of gray appeared. Rising and dropping, the trail followed the river. I stumbled over rocks and roots. When I fiddled with the penlight, it came on again, but its beam seemed alien now. I had light enough to walk by. I squinted at ghostly brush and silhouettes of trees, dry whitish grass, and foggy ferns. The air was damp and woolen, stitched with the fiddle of crickets.

I could make out boulders and deadfall on the path. Though they had browned, blooms of ocean spray unfurled like tide. Mist skeined the river now, wraiths unraveling. In a rapid boulders riddled swaths of foam. First light kindled my spirit and I picked up my pace.

Cut banks bore nature's riprap, a watermark of rocks and moss. The current marked "horizontal" time, but its depth, like the rocky layers of bank, made time vertical, what we wade, dive into, or swim through. Where a creek spilled from a high ledge, I waded through chest-deep sedge to fill my water bottle. Turning to go, I stood eye to eye with a large green locust gnawing a blade of grass. It was about six inches long, bigger than any hopper I'd seen, an elegant, winged chewing machine, avatar of Buddha feasting on green until it *was* green.

89

Tat twam asi.
That art thou.

My watch startled me. I had meant to leave it in the truck. When I slipped it off, a pale ring branded my wrist. A signal of haste and the routine I tried to slough. The woods and river formed a network of living space and time. As city dwellers in industrial culture, we "time" ourselves mechanically—with digital watches, commuter schedules, computer clocks, appointments (the word is telling), and linear routine. The least craving for wildness heartens me. Beneath the artificial tinder of civilization, a spark of primal being smolders, however hard to kindle. We still own animal blood.

The idea that time flows is more than a convenient metaphor. Time is no abstraction but life pulse taking liquid form—sap flowing in the trees, sugars in the leaves, creeks trickling down to the river, which meanders slowly, cascades in a fall, or thunders through rapids. There are imperceptible, manifold flowings. I walked through waves of light. Blood throbbed in my veins. Igneous rocks revealed the liquid strata of geologic time. What the river wore smooth would turn to sand and flow toward a sea where time ran deeper still, its rhythms not just biologic but cosmic. My heart went out to rivers that did not run free, or were dying of humanly infused poisons. And to people who would never fish or walk by water.

As day dawned, I moved to different measures. Limb-filtered light deepened into green. Fern and thimbleberry. Cedar and ninebark. Snowbrush and holly. In the canopy above me, branches opened windows. By midmorning I had caught and released many trout, the native Westslope Cutthroat abundant here. I inadvertently took one life. Casting from a high ledge, I hooked a fish, but didn't get to the bank in time to free it. When I did, the trout drifted belly-up, food for otter, eagle, or an alert raccoon.

The trout's death hurt. I wanted to treat the river as a "thou," the way I felt "it" treated me. It took me as I was, without judgment. Through lack of respect, I had harmed one of its creatures, and in turn it could injure or drown me. Eerie as it was, I wanted to renew the contact I felt in the dark, honor the river, not merely use it.

Sport fishing, like sport hunting, raises ethical questions. Surely a hooked fish suffers. Imagine a steel hook jabs your throat, and you're dragged mouth first out of the water, struggling as life escapes you. Desperate, you gasp and thrash, straining for the breath of home.

Catch-and-release fishing inflicts trauma, and trauma increases mortality. I can't ignore a trout's suffering, only honor it and accept the privilege to engage what otherwise lives unseen. I view trout not as things, but gifts the river gives. At least I try to—when I'm not stumbling on rock slick as ice, getting my line snagged when a fish is on, or muttering "God damn it to hell" when my leader snaps. If I'm lucky I bring the trout close, then let it go. For a second I *see* it as clearly as I can. If fishing feeds my spirit, is the trauma worth it? Does the pain I inflict renew my connection to the natural world, or sever it? The meat fisher wants meat, the sport fisher sport, but I want something else. Suffering triggers my regret, but deepens my respect. Populations in catch-and-release fisheries are abundant and suggest the pain is bearable.

But I rationalize. I might as well be a torturer who keeps his victim alive to lengthen the pain and increase respect. I see the cutthroat drift belly-up, like the fish my father caught that swam in our sink, witness to my fallibility and a friend's advice: "Never underestimate your power to be destructive." It was foolish to fish from that ledge. I should have worked my way down, taken my time, and the river's. Failure turns on should-haves.

A fly fisher wants her fly to mimic insects trout feed on. This way she participates in their world. She lands a fish quickly and releases it while it's in the water. She doesn't seek to harm trout, but to receive them as a gift. After killing that cutthroat, I vowed to temper my eagerness.

Around noon I lay down and dozed against a spindly pine. When I woke, a nickel-sized beetle had landed on my wrist. A brilliant emerald, it may have taken my red ballcap for some exotic flower. Dreaming and waking, we inhabit parallel worlds. The beetle was a gem with legs and wings, whose feelers swayed like

91

metronomes. When I yawned and stretched, it flew off, a speck in the blaze of noon.

A kingfisher veered upriver, scourge of minnow and fingerling. Fish, man, bird, river—each a partner dancing with the others. Together they imply a larger whole, and the whole still others, innumerable, interconnected, and vital in ways as yet unrecognized. They radiate outward to meta-cosmic vibes, and inward, to the still center of a circle. Galaxy to subatomic flicker, quasar to pulse beat. We come and go making our rounds, part of larger, smaller, subtler, ever more intricate orders. Maybe consciousness is a flicker between grit and stars.

᳁

August. Suzanne and I camp on Meadow Creek, a Selway tributary. When I glance up from the camp stove, she sits at the trestle table, chin in her hands. Earlier she picked wildflowers—yarrow, chicory, and cow parsnip, asters still blooming in the dry heat. On the table, arrayed in a Folger's can, they ornament our camp with the many faces of the woods.

But something isn't right. She stands, yanks the flowers from the can, marches to the creek, kneels and tosses them in, one by one. "I think the water needs them," I overhear her say. As blossoms drift away, late sun catches her hair. I know I will remember this moment. What I love is fully present, yet passes away. In less than a month, remaining weeds and flowers will shrivel in frost. Suzanne will be thirteen.

᳁

92   When I dozed a second time, a twinge on my ankle woke me. Humping over sere grass, an ant crawled up my pant leg. As I flicked it away, a western tanager flew across the river. A lemon-scarlet arrow, it landed high in a cedar. It was late afternoon. To get back by dark, I'd have to make time. But hiking at night would be fine too.

On the way back, nothing looked familiar. Last night's solitude had seemed threatening, but now, I felt part of this place. A pool brimmed clear as air, the living room of trout and ouzel. Stones on the bottom shone deep olive and looked magnified, as if the river honed my attention.

Singed by frost, scrub maple hemmed the trail, leaves ocher and gold. Grass was bleached and wheaten, dew no longer enough. Rounding a bend, I met a lone backpacker taking a breather on a log. Bearded, forehead slick with sweat, he sipped a water bottle as he glanced up. Neither of us spoke. The wilderness forged a bond of respect we shared. I nodded as I passed, and he nodded back.

I reached the trailhead near dark. An owl flew across the river and vanished in the trees. It carried the genetic wisdom of its species, a knowledge millennia old. The cells in its body held the current of a living code, a tapestry of genes, climate, and landscape it knew by heart. Or as we say, by *instinct* (literally "pricked" or "touched"), an in-dwelling intelligence our own species often ignores. The owl reminded me of what I could never fully know. My flesh was mostly water, bearing what moved from a source, returning to that source. I sloughed off my pack, walked down to the bank, knelt, and splashed my face. The water in my hands was cold and traceless.

A few hours later as I approached Lewiston, the moon danced on the Clearwater River. When its light caught my hands on the steering wheel, my skin glittered. That hint again. Flecks of trout scale like the river's jewels. In the corner of my eye, current seemed to float the sky. Approaching town in a spangle of ever-changing beams, I caught one and held it for a second. It said earth and sky, mind and river, are one.

Stillness

On I-90 the car rumbled over packed snow. As I squinted through flurries for the fog line, a lake appeared not far from the highway. I only glimpsed it in passing, but the image stayed with me. Kidney-shaped, the size of a putting green, the lake lay beneath snow-shagged ponderosas. In a blink it was gone, a winter moment notched in the scablands of the central Washington plateau.

I had visited my father in Spokane and was driving to Moses Lake for a basketball game. The community college team my youngest son was on would play there that night. I was eager to see Steve, but Dad was on my mind. He lived in a retirement center now and spent most of his day dozing with the TV on. Each month I drove up from Lewiston to visit—take him to lunch, shopping, or do repairs in his apartment. His depression was constant now. And contagious. After two days with Dad, I craved distraction, and it was my luck that Steve had a game I could get to.

An oldies station bled through static, "And I wonder, I wa-wa-wa-wa wu-under . . ." When I switched it off, the image of the lake deepened. Serene at first, like the scene on a winter postcard, it began to grow. By spring the shores would be marshy. Gangs of waterfowl would begin arriving—gulls, avocets, sandpipers, teal, the perennial mallards and gulls. But now, in winter, dead weeds and grasses would crowd the bank, their bleached husks stiff with cold. I imagined frogs tunneled under mud now frozen; perch hovering in suspended animation near the bottom; and crayfish snuggling into crevices of stones. Larva cases of last year's caddis flies, mayflies, and dragonflies lay on snow-fleeced rocks, alongside smaller creatures, dead or dormant now—flatworms, leeches, and countless microorganisms that had cocooned or burrowed in, like time travelers in science fiction, flash frozen for intergalactic travel. The lake was an image of a world apart, a still life in repose. Yet it was also part of me.

I recalled ponds I knew as a boy. They nestled in basalt scabland on the edge of the Spokane valley, remnants of the Great Missoula Flood, when some twelve thousand years ago the world's largest ice dam broke and temporarily drowned eastern Washington. The deluge swept away layers of silt, exposing the slag of volcanic flows. Basalt was my rock of ages. Its eroded turrets and columns flanked the Spokane River, the landscape of my childhood.

In spring, climbing bluffs near my grandmother's house, I nosed ledges hemmed in buttercup and touched the crumbling face of time. It was warm, as if a slow fire burned in stone. Neighbor kids called the place Spring Hill, and I first met stillness there. Standing on the crest, I surveyed the houses below then hiked to a pond where dragonflies sputtered, swallows darted, and frogs croaked.

The ponds weren't always serene. Once two boys with sticks poked at something in the reeds. What looked like a clump of rags became the body of a cat. It was the first dead creature I had seen. Stripped of fur, its skin looked doughy, and the sockets of its eyes bored into me. A voice—whose? The boys weren't talking—said the cat's body would eventually become like the pond. When I think of it now, that Spring Hill cat is a passing cloud. Dragonflies still buzz. Reeds still rustle. And stillness thrives. The ponds were long ago drained and filled for a housing development, but in a blink I'm back there brushing bunchgrass in the mud trails of memory while a breeze tenders the heartbeat of reeds.

·ᴗ

Each morning before light, I sit on a cushion, hands folded, legs crossed beneath me. Holding this position, I close my eyes and focus on my breathing. To say I meditate suggests a control that eludes me. I don't control what happens before light pales the windows. Thoughts, moods, and images—the usual mental junk—bump and jostle. I recollect myself and once more focus on my breathing. If I avoid distractions and let go, I may settle down, and in. In good sessions I don't grasp for what prods, aggravates, or attracts me. I have never felt bliss or ecstasy, whatever they are, but after sitting I feel more centered, more decent to my family, less inclined to self-pity, anger, or the itch for praise.

So I practice stillness. Then I stand, bow, and the day goes on. Routine awareness returns and bangs the door. Sometimes I recall the quiet time of morning and become more mindful, or maybe, in Zen terms, I experience a state of no-mind. Before answering the phone, sealing a letter, or slipping a credit card into a slot, I take a deep breath, let go, and begin.

Stillness can arise involuntarily. When I took my two boys and one of their friends backpacking, we searched for a lake I had spotted on the map. Two hours later, we backtracked along a ridge, still searching. Finally we glimpsed it far down the breaks, a wink of emerald just visible through the woods. There was no trail in sight. "Let's bushwhack down and fish until dark," I coaxed the boys.

We clambered about a hundred yards until the slope got steep. Climbing back would have been as risky as going down. When loose rock gave way in small avalanches, we grabbed pine saplings for handholds until there were none. Now we were in a fix. The lake lay about a hundred yards below, but I had packed no safety cord. If one of us slipped and fell, he'd somersault in a bone-crushing plunge to land on still more rocks below.

We inched along a ledge toward a stretch that looked passable. Bren went first, while Scott and I wedged Steve, Bren's little brother, between us. Thinking would have paralyzed me. It took all I had just to stay on that ledge. Life was groping—toehold by fingerhold, Steve's, my own. Breathe, breathe, and don't look down.

As my adrenaline surged, stillness arrived. I would do anything to keep Steve from falling. *Anything*. I *was* that ledge, right hand clenching rock, left arm my son, inch by harrowing inch. That was all there was to know. And luck was on our side. Seeing our plight, two fishermen below shouted directions to bring us safely

96

down. "See what is before you," says the Zen teacher. "If you have to think, think after the fact. First, know it, be it, let it be you." I still wish I'd brought some safety cord.

Backpacking is an extended lesson in stillness. Lugging fifty-some pounds into high country, I have scant energy for thinking. Things get basic in a hurry. The trail is mind space, the ache in my shoulders, though fierce, increasingly far away. Over time, I move a step ahead of, or behind, my body—in a zone. Backcountry demands clear attention. Routine turns on ritual: gather kindling and keep it dry; light a fire and keep it lit; ration white gas; filter drinking water; fish smart to economize on rations; walk with the readiness of an animal—you can't afford to break a leg out here.

In time the landscape becomes second mind. Woods, a lake, or river aren't scenery, but the contours of your emotions. I don't feel that way about malls, gas stations, or drugstores, or even church, though the almost-tangible light in St. Patrick's Cathedral in New York City opened a hole in the top of my head and let the sky pour through. The nave rises to a vaulted ceiling and the rose window diffuses a spectral blue. It took me back to the woods, my first cathedral. It was as if the sky incarnated through lenses of blue glass. If I ponder the physics of steel, masonry, and concrete, maybe I'll respect the mall too. The vagrant pilfering a dumpster next to Walmart is my *doppelganger*—holiness groping for expression. So Nature, which is also us, begs our blessing.

⤳

The lake by the interstate harbored stillness. Driving, I fretted less. Despite its lid of ice, the lake brimmed inside me. Before I started sitting, I had never experienced positive emptiness. I agreed with a friend who complained about do-nothing types. "Buddhism is a cop-out," he griped. "You drop out, do nothing, empty yourself, and expect to find Nirvana. But, hey, it takes work—you have to give something back." Later, I met real Buddhists and some became friends. They were anything but dropouts. The emptiness they cultivated made them clearheaded, better able to contribute and cope.

Buddhist art celebrates serenity. Depictions of Christ in agony on the cross seem a far cry from placid Gautamas sitting lotus-style, eyes closed, faces blissed. Seeing the Christ of Byzantine mosaics—that calm, centered, wholly inhuman gaze—shocked me at first. But was it really inhuman? Superhuman? Maybe the notion of what's human is the whole point. How far, or deep, do our natural powers go? The gospels say the kingdom of God is within us. A professor of religion once told me that the New Testament expression has rich, but mysterious, meaning. "It's problematic," he said. "You have to explore yourself to find out what it means."

As a boy I explored the river near our house. In its roiling, seaming, and surging, I looked for a pattern. Sometimes I thought I caught it, but then it was gone. When I gazed in soft focus, the currents merged. A trick of the eye, I guessed. Or was it a form of meditation, however crude? The monkey mind became less frazzled. Whittling driftwood had the same effect. When I stayed focused, knife and wood took on a life of their own, distraction fled, and serenity arose. Or emptiness. Or stillness. Nature came naturing. A knot was a snake eye, the fork of a limb a wing. Finally, motion and stillness, change and permanence, meshed, like water flung backward, as in Frost's "West Running Brook":

> The black stream, catching on a sunken rock,
> Flung backward on itself in one white wave,
> And the white water rode the black forever,
> Not gaining, but not losing, like a bird . . .

Maybe Taoists are right. *Chi* is pure energy, the kinetic, electromagnetic, finally ineffable force of the universe breathing. When it's knotted up, we're tight and can't flow. Its power comes not from tension or restriction (as in bodybuilding) but from stretching and loosening. True firmness, the core of muscle tone, is not on the outside, but within. There are eighty-year-old monks so limber they can stretch a leg straight up a wall.

But we live frantically. *I* live frantically. The commute, the daily barrage of e-mail, the committee meeting, the quick lunch and espresso, bits and pieces of a relationship. We suffer surfaces, all rush and clang. And living on the surface atrophies deep mind. Even *in utero*, ultrasound images show the fetus awash in a sloshing thunder. But beneath the range of waves and the pulse of uterine tissue, do still waters buffer the unborn? Maybe we bathe in stillness there, like birds in a warm wind, safe from noise, light, and clamor, our song a merciful heartbeat.

Stillness is rare. Soon enough the drone of the engine and the rumble of tires matched the rigmarole in my head—

> *Steve might be just getting off the bus . . .*
> *Dad is so damned irritable. I'm still the teenager who gets under his skin . . .*
> *Don't wallow in self-pity . . .*
> *My back itches, but I can't reach far enough to scratch ...*

·◡

On the ponds at Spring Hill, I often saw herons. From a distance, I mistook them for snags, exposed roots, or large pendant-shaped weeds. A heron mimics the stillness of the landscape. With ready grace, it collects itself and, propped on a single reedlike leg, like a black belt poised for a kick, waits to spear a fish or frog. Watching herons I had a terrific urge to move. There wasn't much heron in me then—it was hard to stay still for even a minute. Now, maybe, if my life depended on it . . .

99

> *If what's in you holds still long enough, you grow lighter and fly.*

In winter the ponds held greater stillness. Grass stalks were shellacked with ice. Willows drooped like frozen whips, and it felt like I was the only one alive. When pond ice thickened, kids would skate there. By contrast, summer, which I had once thought quiet, was a web of sound—buzz of dragonflies, chitter of swallows, a breeze rustling cattails. In winter, the only sound was my breathing, boots punching snow, or a raven's crawk. My shadow stained the soapy ice. Summer had gone belly-up and lay shrouded in white. There wasn't a bird in sight, and the cold smoked my breath.

Buddhists call meditation "sitting like a frog." It's not a mental state but a bodily disposition. When waves were about to swamp the disciples' boat, Jesus said, "Peace, be still," and the sea obeyed. The disciples had to face their fear, not an actual storm, but the storm within. "Peace, be still" is the pause between breaths, the noiseless center of the wave, or the hush after an owl's cry. It's a heron perched on a rock, waiting for a fish or frog.

When I was teaching my son, Bren, how to fish, he got anxious and his line tangled.

"Relax," I urged him. "You're trying too hard. Don't let your back cast drag."

"Leave me alone. I can do it myself."

After that he gave up, and for the rest of the day, we sulked. Beside a pristine mountain lake, my impatience had wrecked us. It took me years to understand. Now, when anger comes, I breathe deep, let it whale me, then watch it limp away. It works about half the time. Amidst a storm of particles, in throbs of subatomic energy, lies a quiet sea, the Platonic kernel, the emptiness behind Buddha's smile.

100

Last year, I gave Steve a book on Zen. Knowing I practiced, he was curious. As a teenager he had faced anxiety and heartbreak. As a college athlete, he knew the force of discipline. Cheryl and I hadn't been churchgoers, and our attempts to introduce spirituality were piecemeal. We prayed together over meals, told sacred stories, and urged our children to practice kindness and charity. When we could, we taught by example. When we didn't, duty had a hollow ring. The simplest, and hardest, lesson was restraint. "Your sister wanted that Coke. Mom left it just for her." We failed endlessly.

All athletes, our kids discovered "second wind," when they felt they could play forever. Of course, second wind won't last. Starved of oxygen, muscles eventually clutch, the heart gets sluggish and loses its oomph. But staying power abides on the edge of stillness. One moves, or seems to, alongside or out of the body, as close to physical perfection as humanly possible. In mere seconds, an ink-sketch artist catches the soul of an animal or flower, and life's "wind," normally hidden, suddenly presents itself.

Though his hearing was bad and his driving worse, Dad still went to church each Sunday. He went partly out of duty, and partly, I think, out of fear. But the look in his eyes as he watched a sunset showed he could be deeply moved. Once, in a rare moment, he confessed his business career often left him near panic. "There were days when putting one foot ahead of the other was the hardest thing I ever did," he grimaced. He too, I now believe, found stillness. When I saw the lake near the interstate, I quit licking my wounds and began to embrace his. To love him, while I could, for who he was.

As a fisherman, he was drawn to lakes and rivers. He would have admired a poem by William Stafford, a man of his generation, who cultivated stillness too:

Ask Me

Some time when the river is ice ask me
mistakes I have made. Ask me whether
what I have done is my life. Others
have come in their slow way
into my thought, and some have tried to help
or to hurt. Ask me what difference
their strongest love or hate has made.

101

I will listen to what you say.
You and I can turn and look
at the silent river and wait. We know
the current is there, hidden; and there
are comings and goings from miles away
that hold the stillness exactly before us.
What the river says, that is what I say.

That day on I-90, my old self took hold again. I thought of the game and seeing Steve; how I'd find a motel and next morning drive back to Spokane to spend more time with Dad. Things got humdrum. Jetsam, whim, a stray image or mood—what Taoists call "the ten thousand things"—came rushing. If I had remembered Stafford's poem just then, I'd have revised it slightly: "what the lake says, that is what I say."

I took an exit into town—stoplights and traffic, the neon glare of gas stations, restaurants, and motels. Everything was in motion. Soon I'd be sitting in a large gymnasium filled with people. The shuffle of feet and cluck of chatter would crescendo. I would watch Steve warm up and remember when we played H-O-R-S-E in the backyard.

Between breaths, the lake is still. Blue ice floats the sky.

As the game began, I was anxious. The crowd was noisy, the score close. I watched Steve's every move. But stillness was waiting. It came with a sigh. I saw myself—a father on edge, wanting his son to excel, wanting. . . But that sigh took the parental starch, with its sting of ego, out of me. It didn't matter which team won or how well Steve would play. I was here and the challenge was to *be* here, alert, awake, redeeming the nick of time.

102

I waited for a moment that now seemed inevitable: Steve or one of his teammates would let go a perfect shot. The ball would clear the rim in a seamless swish, what players call "nothing but net," followed by cheers and applause. For a moment, the ball would hang like a motionless globe suspended between aspiration and its goal. I might think of my father then, or my wife, daughter, and sons, and count my blessings. If I was lucky, I would catch a glimpse, however faint, of what I was supposed to be doing, and not doing, here, in this busy, noisy world.

Tracks

As I climbed Winchester grade, sleet pasted the windshield. I shifted down, switched on the wipers, and glanced out at the breaks. The canyon wore a blanket of snow and the day was getting colder. Slush on the road was starting to freeze. It was the Saturday before Christmas. Steve and Suzanne were home for college break. The tree was up, presents wrapped, and I was headed for the woods. In the blowing swirls, I scanned the slopes, hoping to spot one of the trestles of the old Camas Prairie Railroad.

In need of a tune-up after a semester of teaching, I was on my way to Winchester Lake. The staff naturalist at the state park there would introduce winter birding and animal tracking. But just then I searched for other signs. Each fall for many years, Cheryl and I took our children to the park to picnic, fish, or hike. As we climbed the grade, they grew excited. Who would be the first to see a trestle? Soon one would holler, "I win," "Firsties," "Bingo," or "Home free."

Where the grade steepened, I trailed a semi spitting slush. When I cleared the truck, the sky seemed to lighten. To my left, above the tree line, cantilevered timbers crosshatched the snow. From the highway the trestle looked like a toy bridge adrift in fog. "Bridge to what?" I wondered. "Hope for my children? For a man declining to age?" As I took the Winchester exit, clouds broke to a patch of blue. Soon, the sky might be clear.

The park field station was a small building nestled against the woods. In the lobby, pamphlets and field guides lay on shelves, and posters of wildlife decked the walls. A print of a bald eagle in flight sported the caption "I'm smiling." After introducing myself to the attendant ranger, I thumbed through picture postcards for sale then looked at fishing regulations. A stack of thank-you cards from schoolkids who had come for field trips held smile-faces and stick figures. They were the day's first tracks. It was good to think of children in the woods, far from bells, computers, and desks. If we need little problem solvers, we also need seers and hearers, who can spot a teal in flight or identify a warbler's cheep.

A jeep pulled up outside, and a sturdy young woman got out, strode briskly into the lobby, pulled off her gloves, and reached for my hand. "I'm Erica, the staff biologist. I'll be your guide." She looked about thirty and wore a heavy parka and hiking boots. Cheeks pinched with cold, she rubbed her hands and huffed, "Good day for a walk." It turned out I was the trip's lone taker.

As we left the field station and walked up a snow-packed road, Erica filled me in. "I was trained in wildlife biology. It's my first love." Her duties included leading field trips, cataloguing flora and fauna, and taking input for a long-range plan. "We juggle competing interests here. Folks come to picnic, camp, canoe, fish, hike, ski, and photograph wildlife. The park is just four hundred acres including the lake. We manage it to improve habitat for animals and birds." Trained in zoology and molecular biology, Erica was a naturalist at heart. "I'm old school by current standards," she said. "I like getting my hands dirty, learning firsthand. You never know what you'll find."

It was a bracing twenty-five degrees, the day after winter solstice. With only a foot of snow on the ground, we made do without snowshoes or skis. When we left the road for a trail along the lake's south shore, Erica took a measured pace, stopping now and again to listen. The woods were still, the lake iced shut, and the sun a pale lozenge hidden in the trees. By noon it would gild ponderosas whose shadows grazed the ice like brushstrokes of charcoal.

The stillness puzzled Erica. "Normally we'd hear siskins, jays, or chickadees. Maybe they fed earlier and are resting, or it's just too cold. I really don't get it." Even the usually boisterous Douglas squirrels were mute. In the distance, a raven crawked, as if someone tried to talk after swallowing a lump of coal. Then silence, our boots punching snow. Suddenly Erica went still. "Was that a frog?"

105

I had heard nothing, but she was confident on this one. "Leopard frogs burrow into mud near the inlet for winter sleep. A tunneler making adjustments must have let go a peep."

To a frog, with its thin, light-sensitive membrane, the cold would feel like ice skin. What if I took off my parka? I imagined cardiac shock and the stupor as circulation slowed. How thick, or thin, was my skin? Or for that matter, my mind? Through snow-clad branches, the day brightened. The stillness of the woods suggested a life beyond the reach of ordinary eyes and ears. Maybe a walk meant thinking in a new way. Or not thinking at all. The monkey mind aside, what could my body know?

With field glasses we scanned pines across the lake for eagles but came up empty. Dense and ever-present, the stillness loomed. Too much talk seemed out of place, as if the woods expected not words but awarenesss. Far off a dog gruffed—a firecracker exploding under a bucket. By now the raven's cry was a half-remembered echo. When we did speak, our voices seemed muted, as if the air had turned solid and muffled their ricochet. In a gap of sky, a contrail slowly dissolved. But Erica wasn't looking up: she knelt beside tracks the size of handprints—large in back, small in front—fan shaped, no sign of claws. "Snowshoe," she bubbled, and the tracks snapped into place. The hare had loped onto the ice, reached the center of the inlet, stopped, and bounded back. On its return, it moved briskly, about five feet per leap. Maybe something startled it—a hawk, fox, snowplow, or our own chatter?

From a footbridge, we saw more tracks loop and zigzag on the snow-covered ice. "Like a jigsaw puzzle," I ventured, "or seams in a quilt," Erica rejoined. Her metaphor was apt. The woods formed a labyrinth of trails and lives. Last night or early this morning, deer had patrolled the frozen cove. Their gait was a "direct register," Erica explained: the rear hoof is placed in the impression of the front, making for surer steps, so the animal doubles its luck. A coyote or wolf moves this way too, but a domestic dog (trained hunting dogs aside) is more slipshod. Guaranteed food and shelter, it can afford to be sloppy.

Whenever I tricked myself into thinking I knew the woods, something would set me straight—flit of an unknown bird, a strange print in clay, a rustle of brush. Here, I was more like a domestic pet myself. Forced to survive outdoors, I'd follow my nose to disaster. Without savvy companions, I'd have to learn from the critters themselves—about food sources, potable water, places to stay warm or hide. Erica never missed a beat. "Those deer must have looked for a drink then circled back when they found the lake iced shut."

Whitman's lines had always moved me: "I think I could turn, and live with animals, they are so placid and self-contained." Of course, he didn't live with animals; he only imagined he could—the crux of "turn." But we shouldn't diminish that. Whitman envisioned how he *might* live. He caught and held the hint of a new reality, or a very old one.

But as much as I admire cougars or wolverines, I'm a creature who thinks. Often too much. Old fashioned know-how might help me change a spark plug, find a tax loophole, even talk someone out of killing himself, but my thinking is more apt to be abstract and displaced. There can be value in that, too, but it tends to distance life rather than embrace it. That day in the woods, something more Whitman-like began to occur. Given time, tutoring, and effort, could I bring animal powers into the range of thinking? What sort of life might an animal possess? For a moment I intuited a thinking that isn't abstract, in the ordinary way, but which, without bias, with openness and honesty, ponders the inner being of another life, or kind of life. Listening and seeing converged with snow, tracks, and Erica's ears and eyes. Lichen draping pines hovered like the smoke of remembered fires.

107

⌐

Indian summer. A warm afternoon. On the trail our toddlers lag behind us. They're poking, snooping, and maundering like little ones do. When something gets their attention—a snapped limb, dried grass or needles, a pinecone or pebble—they pick it up, inspect it, carry it a while, then drop it again. They make friends and let them go. We surprise a garter snake sunning in dry grass—a whiplash and gone. The red-tailed hawk I hope for—the one we saw last year?—scouts from a ponderosa, on the lookout for squirrel, mouse, or vole.

The scene is a fall pastoral: leaves of *Ceanothus* and ninebark mingle reds and yellows, and some have fallen on the path. Clumps of bunchgrass look sere as broomstraw. The trail merges with an old logging road flanked by second-growth pine. When it opens into a meadow, a figure approaches us. A boy, twelve or thirteen, wearing jeans and sneakers, naked to the waist. His dark skin and black hair say he's Nez Perce. In one hand he carries a spinning rod; in the other, dangling from a stick, a hefty trout. "How's it going?" I ask. He nods but doesn't speak. Under a tough veneer, he seems vulnerable. When he passes, I walk in his tracks.

He may live on the reservation, at Lapwai, where alcoholism, drug addiction, and unemployment are epidemic. Did an elder teach him old ways—respect for living beings, how to fish, dance, and drum? He looks askance at the white family entering these woods. To him we're tourists, not people who belong. Maybe he comes by his wariness naturally, through blood memory, the story of displacement, violence, and loss.

A moment ago, I felt we belonged here. But seeing this boy recalls the lessons of history—broken promises and treaties, lies, havoc, and genocide. What to do? Support the American Indian College Fund, attend powwows, shake hands with an elder? I don't know. Understand, would seem to be a minimal, if demanding, requirement. To do it I'd have to strip away much of what I am. Watching the boy go saddens me. I don't know him, but I want to.

Aboriginal cultures are vital to us. As languages wither and elders die, a few brave souls work to honor their memory: of hunting and gathering; bartering and vision quests; trade routes and customs, intimacy with animals and land; spiritual rites and bonds. Honoring these cultures we're far from corporate board rooms, call centers with hundreds of computer screens, the aridity of academic committees, or the drudgery of assembly lines. We are lost in a good way, with hope of snapping into place.

In an age of scientific ecology, environmental initiatives, and the politics of conservation, it may seem trite to speak of "mother earth." We may romanticize the life of the Indian. But it's treacherous to forget these histories, and the role our ancestors and their descendents played in them. What was that life, from tribe to tribe, culture to culture, really like, and how can we honor it? Is it possible for white people, with white consciousness, using white language, to fathom it?

Canoeing the lake in another spring, I thought of the boy again. He had seemed vulnerable to our presence, but also part of the place, like a turtle sunning on a snag, or coots and mallards dabbling among the reeds. I remembered his eyes darting away and back. He was wary, but not tense. Surely, he was like my own sons—worried about making the basketball team or being too shy ever to attract a girl. Do I project on him a third-hand image of Indianness? I don't know. I only say what I felt. What happened *before* I thought. This was years ago and I see him still.

.⤙

The air was crystalline and exact. If it had had a mouth, it might have spoken volumes. Erica felt there was something to the stillness. "Maybe stiffer cold, a front moving in, or more snow," she guessed. "Maybe it has to do with solstice, the shortest day of the year." I thought of the life buried around us—the lacework of roots; nodes of bacteria and webs of fungus dormant now; water slowed to a crawl or frozen as it percolated through loam to bedrock; the somnolent gnawings of insects, rodents, and birds that were awake, and the dormancy of others, folded under the snow. Maybe the woods did speak, but we were ill equipped to hear.

Except for gray patches where current ran beneath it, the ice was solid. Deer tracks proved it. Soon huts of ice fishers would dot the lake like houseboats. Smoke from their fire buckets would make it look like a campground. As recently as 1963, a saw mill stood on the north shore. In those days the town of Winchester, Idaho, named for the rifle maker, was a logging community of some seven hundred souls. The lake is manmade. Originally a holding area for logs, it's now forested on the west and south shores. Here silviculture revives what extractive culture diminished. On the east shore, the collapsed timbers and rusted winches of a slaughterhouse lay rotting in the snow. As we walked, I imagined the grumble of machinery and the bawling of cattle whose ghosts seemed to haunt the hills.

Erica knelt again. Some small creature had skittered from hiding near the trail. "A vole, I think—no: white-footed mouse!" Maybe the creature had dragged food back to its den—a leaf with some viable pigment or a grass blade it found, still partly green. Four-toed in front, five-toed behind, its track held a central groove engraved by its tail, as if a tiny, three-legged skier had left its hieroglyphic. It didn't leap like the snowshoe, but moved with a lippeting hop, leaving symmetrical tracks, like the outlines of serrated leaves. Its rear claws helped it cling to tree bark when it climbed. The creature made its way in a dangerous world. Fox, coyote, and owl lived here too. Whether guests or inhabitants, nesters or intruders, we leave our tracks.

Erica and her husband lived in a cabin near the lake. He was the caretaker of the nearby wolf interpretive center, where the public could observe captive gray wolves transplanted from Yellowstone National Park. At night the couple fell asleep to a chorus of yips and howls. They taught visitors how to value wild places and creatures. And they lived close to the land. Their cabin had no electricity or plumbing. They cut wood for heat and drove to town twice a week for showers. Their life held rewards not found in a society that esteems physical comfort and artificial pleasures. In small but vital ways, they'd leave their mark here.

·⤳

Tracks are the script of nature's memory. They mark intersections of surprise. A few years back a friend and I led a field trip on the edge of the Selway-Bitterroot Wilderness. Students sketched, took field notes, and wrote journal entries. John introduced forest ecology and the diversity of species. I talked about wilderness and the American mind. On the way back, a woman big with child had trouble keeping up. As I walked with her, we fell behind the main group. "How's the pregnancy going?" I asked. "It's my first," she said shyly. "I've had a little morning sickness. It's a boy."

A few yards ahead something darted across the trail. It was tawny and quick, probably a deer. I told the woman to wait and went on for a look. A moment later, I was staring into the eyes of an Idaho mountain lion. Just heading into the woods, it turned and looked straight at me. Only a lunge separated us. I thought of the woman a short way back. The lion must have hidden near the creek we followed, waiting until our group had passed, then, thinking it was alone, recrossed the trail toward higher ground. It hadn't expected a pair of stragglers. When the cat flattened its ears and hissed, I braced myself. But it turned and strode quickly into the brush. When I told the mother-to-be, she frowned and we hurried to catch the others.

Later I showed John a track the cat had left. He studied it, grinned, stared wistfully toward the woods, then back at the print. "Yup, it's cougar all right. Maybe three inches heel to toe, four-toed, with claws retracted. This one's a rear print, I think." None of us had a camera that day. I can still see John's smile, the far look in his eyes.

111

I had nearly canceled the field trip. My first grandchild was about to be born. At the last moment I chose to go, thinking I'd be back in time. As near as I can tell, my granddaughter arrived when the cougar appeared. Now she and the cat are woven into memory, a dreamtime in which animal and human mesh. I see the track in clay, in my granddaughter's eyes. Other lives inform us.

·᠕

A lifetime ago, on river sand, I scrawled pictures with a stick. I made circles and waves, conjuring sun and water, like a would-be shaman carving petroglyphs. A few years later, I carved initials on the wall of our garage to see if a girl at school would smile back. Writing now, I lay down the tracks of words. Though the alphabet from which the letters derive was originally pictographic, the life these words reflect isn't in the actual script, but in its larger resonance. In the woods there are many texts—what Gary Snyder calls the stratigraphy of trees, the calligraphy of rivers, and the cryptography of stones. At Winchester Lake, Erica taught me to read still others. The park was a scriptorium in which nature had written its many names.

·᠕

The tracker and the tracked. As a small boy I followed my father while he fished, but lost sight of him in high brush. I couldn't see the bear, but it saw me. I could taste its breath and feel its fur bristle. I was too young to be afraid. A moment later I stumbled onto a scat pile steaming in the grass. Was I tracking the bear or the bear me? Then I *felt* it vanish into the woods. It's one of my earliest memories. When my father disappeared, the bear took his place, like an elder I had to follow. That bear tracks me still.

Recently, in a remote river canyon, I found bear tracks on a sandbar where I fished. They were small, probably a yearling's. The clearest was palm shaped, a tapered horseshoe, etched in the damp sand. The five toe pads formed an arc, the claw tips razor

112

sharp. The track was clear and fresh. I felt the bear pause and stare at the water. There, beside a fast-moving stream, a hieroglyphic breathed.

I stood and began casting. The stream was about ten yards across. When I glanced up, the print came awake. From a ledge above the far bank, the bear sat watching me. The yearling was curious but wary. "It doesn't get any better than this," I thought, "fishing and bear watching at the same time." But my cast startled the black. In a flash it skedaddled, covering forty yards of canyon slope in seconds.

·ــ

Tracking requires factual know-how, but also imagination. You look down and around as you walk, and the ground is a map. In time, you may sense the bird or animal whose track you mark. A tracker takes the bearings of life unseen, often unknown. In time, tracking may become an exercise in seeing what isn't there. When I found the yearling blackie's track in sand, an electric charge ran through me. Everything I had heard, seen, or read about bears seemed to converge, as if a little bear bomb exploded in me. The phenomenologist Merleau-Ponty writes: "Meaning is invisible, but the invisible is not contradictory of the visible: the visible itself has an invisible inner framework, and the in-visible is the secret counterpart of the visible."

I'm an amateur at tracking, but something always asks to be noticed. It's a matter of learning to read. A fisher reads the water, a farmer the weather. The habit of bare attention bolsters routine understanding. It's a kind of listening within. When Cheryl gets quiet and picks at her eyebrow, something's troubling her. Years have taught me better than to ask, "What's the matter?" She has to live with it awhile, bear it until a felt understanding grows. In time, she'll be ready to talk, and I won't have to ask.

113

·ــ

Circling back toward the field station, we crossed another deer trail. The oldest trails are those of predator after prey or critters after water. Animals, and their stories, first taught us our way. In these parts Coyote was once lord. Where the trail intersected a park road, dog tracks appeared. Some may have belonged to Coyote. It would be like him to camouflage his signs.

While Erica listened for birds, I inspected deer scat. The droppings were dark and sinewy. "Sign of a late year diet," she noted. "Dry pebbly stuff, not easy to digest, like bark or roots." In spring when succulents appear, the scat would be softer, massed together. Erica read the language of scat, syllables in the lexicon of whitetail. Recently, she'd spotted a doe with twin fawns. Tracks she'd noticed elsewhere in the park said they'd wintered here.

When sun rifled gaps through the trees, a gust of wind showered us with glitter. Why is it beauty hurts? How does seeing something outside trigger wonder within? If we respond to patterns, why do some patterns make us rejoice, others rend us, and some do both at once? We've barely begun mapping the interplay of human and nonhuman orders, the dance of that larger mind.

There was much we didn't or couldn't see. On a bird walk, we saw no birds. Apart from the raven, we heard none. "I could have scheduled the walk earlier in December," Erica mused, "but there'd have been no snow. Trackwise, we've been lucky." A few winters back she spotted a ruby-crowned kinglet, a bird the size of a golf ball, rarely seen. She was inspired but took no pride in it. "You get the best views of wildlife when you aren't looking for them. You just anticipate. What counts is clear attention." So Erica was a philosopher to boot. All day I sensed things I wasn't sharp enough to take in.

As the field station came into view, a dog was barking. Maybe it had spotted a deer or heard our voices. I thanked Erica for taking me along. "I learn something each time," she smiled. "Those snowshoe tracks were the best I've seen." We shook hands. I wished her well and told her the park had a good friend.

The croak of the raven stayed with me. An omen neither good nor bad, it *meant* without words. The silence remained, but I was part of it now. I wondered if my children had heard it. When the naturalist Edwin Way Teale was a boy, his grandfather took him on a winter wood-cutting trip in the forests of northern Indiana. For Teale, the silence lasted a lifetime: "Behind and beyond the silence and inactivity of the woods, there was a sense of action stilled by our presence; of standing in a charmed circle where all life paused, enchanted, until we passed on." The experience left Teale with an endless curiosity about the woods and its creatures, and so the instinct of a naturalist was born.

I left the park at noon under sky threatening snow. On a bend where the lake came into view, I spotted a bird flying across the ice. It was already far off, hard to see in the returning overcast. Its plumage was dark, maybe black. Was it the raven? I stopped, switched off the engine and rolled down the window. No sound— only the silence of cold and snow. I knew the woods only seemed to be sleeping. Under the snow, life went about its business. The bird grew smaller against the horizon, then vanished into gray sky over the far shore. I wondered where it might be going.

The Parlors of Heaven

In September, I hanker for blackberries. On a warm afternoon, I fetch a bucket from the basement, climb our fence, and cross a field to a patch that sprawls near the road. If Cheryl wants to bake, I make several trips. Otherwise I put the berries on oatmeal, blend them into a shake, or savor them by the raw handful. And I'm in good company: ants clamber up the vines, and moths, bees, wasps, yellow jackets, and a sometime sparrow or two putter among the rust-singed leaves.

The patch is so thick I can't wade far, but other visitors have left signs—moth wing, fleece of a rabbit or fox, and on the ground a snake's shed skin. When I squat and peer into the undergrowth, vines form a labyrinth of sun and shade. If I could shrink to snake size, I'd slip in for a nap. The interior is off limits to pickers, though I can imagine getting tangled. If I hacked in with a machete, I could end up like the yellow jacket I found trapped in a half-eaten berry. It flailed feebly, doing a backstroke in a sticky tomb.

Blackberry picking is a lesson in restraint. Success means enduring the afternoon sun, staying nimble-fingered, and curbing your appetite. My gallon Folger's can rarely gets full, and given the hunger of imagination, the largest berries are the hardest to reach. I suffer nagging and scratching, but usually fail to get at them. Maybe that's why, during the Middle Ages, blackberry picking was a metaphor for damnation.

I first picked blackberries on the Washington coast. They were Himalayans, moisture-loving natives of Eurasia, whose name suggests the exotic and remote. While my wife and in-laws were shopping, I borrowed a bucket and walked to a thick patch. As I picked I stumbled onto a box someone must have thrown from a car. It contained magazines, some of whose wind-torn pages were caught among the thorns. I stood in a gallery of women, their skin no longer glossy, but rain crinkled and flecked with mold.

The starlets of pornography had met their comeuppance in a berry patch. In a reversal of the usual trend—civilization stomps nature—the lure of consumer lovelies signaled ruin. Nudes of the studio were crumpled and faded. Our human business on the planet seemed ephemeral just then—desire for sale, overrun with vines.

Berry picking is a full-meal deal. You get scratched, scraped, pricked, and so juiced up you look like the victim of a firing squad who somehow survived. Squelchy as offal, the berries in your bucket ooze and fester. A bramble marks nature, you included, at its scrappiest. It rambles, spires, and aspires, sprawls to claim ground, and rewards those who stick to it. Picking is a palatal and digital delight. It links us to earth's mystery and its gifts.

I pick berries less often now. Our children are grown; family berry expeditions are history, and demands at work take up more of my time. Budget cuts, a heavier teaching load, and learning new technologies conspire. I get outdoors less often, and technology, rather than saving me time, requires more of it. In early fall, instead of berry picking, rambling, or fishing, I'm apt to be tapping a keyboard, blinking at a screen, or deleting reams of e-mail, the info-pablum that comes with being "connected." I thought I'd be in the swim with hi-tech by now—I've used computers for years—but too often, ambushed by the latest electronic time-saver or "speeder-upper" (was it Adobe PageMaker last month?), I long for berry picking.

The other day at work, on my way down the hall, I passed offices—five in all—whose doors were open. In each office a colleague sat glued to a computer screen. Seeing them in identical poses with identical equipment gave me pause. Bugs stuck to flypaper came to mind, and I knew I was stuck too. Each day over the past decade or so, I've gotten more wired, become more of a tapper, blinker, and gazer. I'm like the worshipper of an electronic god. I sit before the sanctum of a lit screen and with the punch

117

of a prayer button receive information from a virtual infinity of sources that blip, bleep, dance, flicker, and transform themselves before my eyes. In short, I'm a pawn of the electronic age.

After my little epiphany, I recalled former pleasures: a faculty lunch-bunch where colleagues discussed things literary and philosophical; a walk to the registrar's office to hand over a grade sheet—the paper kind—and have a brief chat with the clerk (a small college, ours); the now almost prehistoric intimacy of flipping through a card catalogue to see what might show up. (There was a sense of quiet camaraderie in fingering the smudgy prints of countless unknown bookworms or students doing desperate last-minute searches). And best of all were the lunch breaks I took. I'd grab a folder of student essays, get a sandwich at the union, and walk to a small park overlooking the river. There I'd sit, muse, stare, chew, smell the spruce trees, and read at my leisure. Those times were so pleasant I never thought of them as "grading."

Now I need more time to answer and delete e-mail and to "process" information—as distinguished from parlaying ideas and speculations or conversing with an actual, instead of virtual, person. A grouchy Luddite? Perhaps. Or a die-hard blackberry picker who flounders in a wired-up world. I advise students online, record grades online, do research online, "teach" a course online, receive memos, instructions, gossip, grants, and committee reports online, and try to keep pace with Web sites I increasingly associate with cancer cells.

Not so long ago, life seemed less grim and purpose driven. I would have witnessed a more diverse scene in the hall. One colleague would have been reading a (bound) book; another chatting on the phone; another talking with a student—face-to-face; a fourth scribbling on a notepad (yes, paper), and a fifth plunking a typewriter. By the late eighties or early nineties, some, but not all, of the offices would have contained a computer, but it wouldn't yet have been on center stage. What struck me that day was how radically things had changed in a short time.

The physiological affects of prolonged computer use are well documented. I've experienced many of the symptoms—shoulder and wrist pain, carpal-tunnel twinges, eyestrain, more frequent headaches, and bouts of nervous agitation. It may seem passé now to complain about computers, which are standard fixtures everywhere. But the problems run deeper than is normally admitted and may raise issues about the conditioning of perception, even of mental health.

Are computers really liberating devices? In many ways they constrain us. Computers enforce the tyranny of binary logic (try to find a keystroke for "maybe") and condition us to the glare of artificial light at close range. They teach us to value speed and efficiency and to focus on fast-moving visual stimuli. *Click-click / drag-click / scroll-click / delete-delete-delete* become a machinelike finger talk that betrays a frame of mind. By comparison, using a typewriter, if you're lucky enough to own one, is direct and simple. With computers, "truth" appears at a touch, borne on a current that titillates, as if a genie in the PC or laptop had cast a spell. Maybe a genie has. I'd rather go berry picking.

I acknowledge the opposition. Not knee-jerk technological fundamentalists, who think I'm nuts, but reflective folks who by choice, necessity, or both, use computers often. I recognize that these machines allow quick access to information, some of which is useful, and that they make some mechanical tasks less daunting. I know, too, that computers can offer a more level playing field in the economy and in political enfranchisement, though those who control the wealth and power still count for most. The real issues, I believe, run deeper. Computer use causes us to abolish, forget, or ignore skills and habits we once, with good reason, held vital.

Recently a student came in to talk over an essay she was writing. We spoke quietly, exchanging personal anecdotes, questions, and insights. I'd read a stretch, ask a question or make an observation, and she'd respond. We enjoyed a provocative exchange. She wrote about a strained relationship with her mother. It was her attempt to sort through murky feelings, see more clearly who her mother was and how she, the writer, now in middle age, still saw herself through her mother's eyes. Our talk moved from matters of style to her own coming of age. We danced around, through, and into the subject. Insights raced along, slowed down, returned, and deepened. By increments, through detours and recirclings, with courage and insight, she was finding her voice—her articulate awareness of herself and memories that challenged her.

Since the advent of computers and their networks, such an experience, though perhaps always rare, has become exceedingly so. It could never be duplicated online or through videoconferencing, and surely not on a telephone. Our contact was immediate. It had spunk and electricity—the kind that requires no plug or cord. Gender notwithstanding, there were moments it seemed we shared each other's emotional histories.

Nowadays the temptation to forget this kind of exchange is strong. E-mail and texting seem easier, quicker, and more convenient, but what glitters isn't always gold. For the current generation, electronic "communication" is second nature. It's so pervasive folks will be hard pressed to realize there are other options, often simpler and more intimate. What happens when you put an ear to the ground, or look directly, and humbly, into another's eyes?

While electronic media transfer data rapidly, they diminish, distort, silence, or reduce direct contact, where people open up face-to-face, as breathing, bodily beings. Whether consciously or not, we intuit the aura of facial expression, physical gesture, and the suasions, depths, and aversions of the eyes. We speak and breathe in a field of energy both tangible and hidden. Such sharing, whether mercurial or heartfelt, doesn't occur on a plastic screen, but is part of a direct, vital exchange, one that's strained and diminished when an artificial mediator gets in the way, especially one as invasive and comprehensive as a computer,

120

which dictates not only what and how we remember, but how we express ourselves.

Recently a nurse complained to me. Instead of writing a report at the end of her shift, she must now carry a hand-sized computer, follow the doctor on his rounds, and record data quickly. "We nurses don't even talk to each other anymore," she frowned. I thought of self-service checkout stations at markets and stores. I need not waste my time chatting with or thanking a live clerk—I can rush right through. I haven't experienced psychotherapy by PC, but I question the logic that sees the presence of a human therapist as invasive. I admire my doctor, but he pays less attention to me now. He hurriedly enters my issues on his laptop, reviews data from my last visit, and updates it. I want him to look me in the eye, take my pulse himself (instead of having the nurse do it), and ask, "How's it going, really . . . ?"

In an electronic culture what I shared with my student, a fact of the human situation for millennia, is speeded up, depersonalized, reduced to hyperspace, or lost entirely. And the list of gadgets grows apace, as do the temptations of ease, speed, and efficiency that make them seem indispensable. Newspapers, infomercials, films, and TV once formed a fringe of our consciousness, but they were never on center stage. During the sixties television began to consume us. To this now add video games, virtual reality toys, cell phones, Game Boys, iPods, computers of all shapes and sizes, and a society wired to an ever-shifting network of artificial information, and the result is patent: psychic and cultural overload. It may be no accident that the heyday of computer marketing and development in the eighties and nineties was accompanied by an explosion of mood-altering drugs. Now Paxil, Prozac, and their spin-offs share equal footing with caffeine as fingers dash over keys and eyes blink at computer screens.

I'm part of the problem. I use a computer too. As a writer fond of pen, paper, and typewriter, I was skeptical when the first word processors appeared. A bookworm as well, I saw the enemy lurking behind a screen. (As I write, electronic "books" are upon us). The computer wasn't just a fancy typewriter. It was a machine competing for a whole range of sensibilities and skills that were once simple to apply, but whose content and expression were subtle. Learning the loops, slashes, dots, and crosses of cursive script, a child experienced the physicality of semantic history, from the days of the earliest writing—carving on wood or stone—to the advent of other relatively simple writing instruments. Nowadays, we experience language as bodiless and voiceless, mediated by what flashes on, and vanishes from, a plastic screen.

The computer brought its own language, one using shortcuts and shorthand, in which abstract—essentially mathematical— commands replaced actual words and the handiwork of fingers, pens, scissors, paste, and paper. Years ago, fiddling with (and being admonished by) my first computer, I sensed what Sven Birkerts would later call "the argument between technology and the soul." His view that electronic culture has turned us away from the depth of inner experience to the "ersatz security of a vast lateral connectedness" is now so patent it's virtually (pun intended) unseeable. Increasingly, the mental and emotional equipment to make the distinction is lost to us. Isn't it possible that the change we're undergoing, the onrush of data and gadgets that process and disseminate it, creates not just overload, but a diminished version of human beings?

The cult of information turns us into hurry machines. Increasingly, we deal with surfaces and techniques, not the centered calm of reflection. I can muse before my computer, but when I turn to key tapping, the urge to rush revives, in a way it never seemed to when I used a pen or typewriter. Both oral and print cultures moved at a slower pace, whether folks were talking, reading, or writing. People saw life less as a play of surfaces, and more as a field with vertical depth, where work, play, story, and ceremony informed each other. When she plied a camas meadow with a stick along with members of her family, having first given thanks to the spirits, and recalled a story, a Nez Perce woman not only dug roots and helped earth breathe; she partook of the rhythms of the cosmos itself. In an electronic culture, what will speed and efficiency buy us? What habits, moods, and inclinations do I feed my ever-rushed soul? However melodramatic it may seem, the notion of a Faustian pact may not be so far-fetched.

I confess a fetish—an obsessive love, even lust, for the printed page. I can hold, touch, finger, and turn it, forward and back. It's flesh of my flesh, squeezed and bleached from the pulp of trees. I lament losing the text to electronic flimflam. On a word processor, the page, originally analogous to the leaf—a finite, discrete, organic medium—dissolves into electronic soup. Text, from *texere*, "to weave," recalls the making of paper from woven strips of papyrus and the notion that composing in words was a form of weaving. On a computer, words aren't residual signals of meaning—a volatile truth—but bits of *disjecta membra* soon to be rearranged or erased. A "text" message is bytes on a computer chip or pixels on a screen. The script of the disembodied soul.

Cultural jargon spawned by computers has blurred crucial distinctions. Do we really enter a "global village," that McLuhan oxymoron, or experience "multidimensional reality?" I'm told I can interface with Russians or Fiji Islanders, stroll through the Louvre to vivid splashes of color, or play odds with the Dow Jones, all in the same afternoon. But to do it I must spend hours at a desk, staring at a plastic screen and tapping keys as I ponder the flicker of the virtual world, which comes at me constantly and demands my fixed attention increasingly. Not to mention what was once obvious: I'm not really *in* the Louvre or Russia, and not in face-to-face contact with an actual, as opposed to virtual, person or place in the world. Each day the question "What's the difference?" finds fewer able to answer.

123

･ﾉ

Enter 9/11. After the initial shock, I was confused and uncertain. The event was so overplayed in the media that my feelings were blunted. Watching the towers plummet in flames for the umpteenth time, I felt dulled, even bored. The networks' high-pitched drama insulated me from an essential truth: the force of the event on those who performed it and those who suffered it. I needed to mourn, but the rush of artificial images thwarted me. I couldn't express what I couldn't, or didn't know how to, feel. I could neither ignore the event, nor deal with it.

Thinking only made it worse. I couldn't join the debate, which became blatant in its extremes. Some gloated about how we deserved it (greedy corporate superpower gets its comeuppance) while others jawed for revenge. Something profound had happened, but I couldn't—wouldn't?—face it. I wanted to blame corporations, Muslim extremists, even technology. People in the twin towers used computers that linked them to a "global economy"—a crowning abstraction, whose truth betrays capitalism's grip. Increasingly, the only thing that binds us is money and the technology to transfer or exchange it. Other technologies and our willingness to make them accessible (in flight training, flight plans and destinations, maps, floor plans, even box cutters) made it easier for the terrorists to succeed.

Our own security systems may have failed because of overload. Electronic snooping generates so much data, so densely layered, that few can navigate it. The politics of bureaucracy, with its specialization and turf wars, thwarts those who might otherwise persuade us as to the risks we face. In the case of 9/11, computer fixation in the defense and security sectors may have bred tunnel vision fostered by reams of data, which arrived out of context, clogging the system and the minds of those trying to process it.

But there was more. The year after the attack, I was at loose ends. As the date drew near, I needed to commemorate it, but the water was murky. September 11 was our daughter Suzanne's birthday. A sophomore in college, working part-time, she was in

124

debt. She had missed enough rent payments and work that her landlord and employer put her on notice. Thinking her trouble temporary, I had sent money more than once. Cheryl intuited deeper problems, but Suzanne didn't want to talk. "I'm fine, Mom, just going through a tough time," she rejoined. Later, Cheryl and I quarreled about it.

"You brood too much. She's a good kid, she'll get through this. It's just a matter of time."

"You throw money at her, but you won't stare trouble in the face."

One night after she called Suzanne, Cheryl was visibly shaken. "Something's really wrong. I can hear it in her voice. There's no feeling in it. She sounds goofy and distracted." That night I dreamed Suzanne had fallen into a vat of molten liquid that flickered under neon lights. Air bubbles showed she was breathing, but she couldn't swim to the surface. The heat came from her own body. She was drowning in liquid fire.

When I told Cheryl about the dream, she called Suzanne again. Cheryl pressed hard and finally the truth came out. After having her wisdom teeth pulled, Suzanne was in severe pain. Several rounds of painkillers and antidepressants helped, but when she went back to work, she was hooked. She got more painkillers from a friend, and from there, junkies and binge-drinking entered the scene.

Cheryl was a wreck; I wallowed in guilt. Suzanne agreed to get counseling, and we agreed to pay for it. Cheryl had been right. I couldn't see far, or deep, enough. Or wouldn't. The shadow that obscured vision was in my own eye. That September, anxious and worried, I decided to go blackberry picking.

On a warm afternoon I left town, passed the industrial park, and turned onto a dirt road skirting the Snake River. I remembered a berry patch where our family had picked and picnicked years before. I parked by a brushy field, clambered over a wire fence, and crossed a rail bed banked in mulberry. The brush was so high

125

it hid the river from view. I searched for remnants of that day years before—a plastic baggie, a scrap of shoelace, a bottle cap that got away. But brambles had overrun the place. Nothing looked familiar. I couldn't even find our picnic spot and was about to turn back when a deer trail headed toward the river beckoned.

I was too late for berries. In the heat, they had shriveled to a crisp on the vines, like gumdrops on a July sidewalk. When I finally saw the river, something had changed. Bluffs on the far bank were doing headstands, but it wasn't their reflection I saw. Instead, I witnessed the world's inverted image. The rubble of the twin towers smoldered in my gut. I thought of Cheryl and the boys, of Suzanne's despair, and of strangers who grieved. I had been eager to cast blame—on corporate greed, evangelical chauvinism, the *realpolitik* of oil. I blamed myself for Suzanne's addiction, but fled my own grief. Coming back to the berry patch was a diversion. What had I expected to find? Did I really think that berry picking would make things right again?

· ✦

A few weeks later, I reread Whitman's "Song of Myself"—

> *I believe a leaf of grass is no less than the journey-work of the stars,*
> *And the pismire is equally perfect, and a grain of sand, and the egg of*
> *   the wren,*
> *And the tree-toad is a chef-d'oeuvre for the highest,*
> *And the running blackberry would adorn the parlors of heaven,*
> *And the narrowest hinge in my hand puts to scorn all machinery,*
> *And the cow crunching with depress'd head surpasses any statue,*
> *And a mouse is miracle enough to stagger sextillions of infidels,*
> . . . .
> *I find I incorporate gneiss, coal, long-threaded moss, fruits, grains,*
> *   esculent roots,*
> *And am stucco'd with quadrupeds and birds all over,*
> *And have distanced what is behind me for good reasons,*
> *But call any thing back again, when I desire it.*

What I had searched for that day on the river finally came to me. As I read aloud, Whitman's lines evoked the natural world freshly perceived, what the speed and flash of artificial data never give me. The experience was dense, pleasurable, and layered, mentally and physically. The interplay of consonants and vowels—"fruits, grains, esculent roots"—wove feeling and thinking together. Whitman's sounds and rhythms offered rich mouth-feel. The consonants are varied (fricatives, velar and dental stops, sibilants, and liquids like *n, l,* and *r*) and the vowels (*oo—ea—oo—oo*) evoked physical pleasure—I could almost taste the words. As they took voice, the surf-roll of phrases measured my breathing. Words came to life in my throat, and in the memory and renewed contact with a place my family had loved.

What triggered all this wasn't just print on a page, but what Whitman and I brought to it. My grief for Suzanne, my frustration with technology, the tragedy of 9/11, and a remembered berry expedition flowed together. The berries I hadn't picked were tantalizing presences. Whitman's poem was a bramble in which words grew, and their meaning held a delicious, if bittersweet, aftertaste. The book pressed lightly into my hand, I could smell the ink and bleach in the paper, even a slight must of decay (the edition was many years old). The word *meaning* hardly covers it. What I experienced wasn't merely intellectual, but whole. It encompassed beauty—the delicacy of blossoms—and pain—the pricking of thorns. And finally, wonder, that life could be so fierce and vulnerable at the same time.

Whitman's "meaning" was a field of impressions, a contact both rich and panoramic, and free of mere ego attachment. We *are* the upshot, or downfall, of what's around and within us, respect for which is born of seeing, praise for which is born of saying. We are free to imagine and to let go, "call any thing back again, when I desire it." We incorporate within us all the elements of nature, and to recognize this is to find contact with a cosmos that, however strange or mysterious, is not alien but home.

That day on the river I had sunk into self-pity, but reading Whitman brought me to my senses. Compared to that of electronic media, the experience was rich as berry picking. Read on a computer screen, Whitman's poem would be hosted by the intermediary of a plastic world, with all its associations, and my pleasure and contemplation dulled. There's something quietly intimate about holding a book and letting it speak. What I "called back," finally, was Suzanne, and how Cheryl and I loved her. We were powerless. We had done all we could. Recovery was in our daughter's hands.

·~

Electronic culture brings us closer only superficially, through a barrage of artificial images and a rush of data. Habitual computer use removes us from direct contact with nature—the earth and our own bodies—and highlights the buzz and flash of a surface-bound connectivity. But what connects us most deeply? Cruising through endless data and Web sites is, finally, an exercise in oblivion. Computer use promulgates a machinelike habit of mind.

Ingenious and quirky, vital yet finite, the mind works best for those who are grounded. For the gurus of artificial intelligence, it may be an ocean of infinite contexts, rapid-fire association and feedback, a grid of endless binary options and surface stimuli. But here I falter. I don't pretend to know what the mind is, though I sense its intricate involvement and coevolution with the body and the earth. What, in fact, are mind and body, and the subtle nexus between? How can we nurture them, and each other?

Think of images of what it has meant, to be human: a reaper in a field of grain; a knight on his steed; a woman grinding corn; a funeral procession or wedding feast; a mother giving birth. Now think of images of the individual in solitude: Rodin's *The Thinker,* Michelangelo's *David,* depictions of the goddess Athena or of a Masai woman carrying a basket on her head. All turn on the interplay of bodily energy and inner repose. Now compare two images: a woman reading a book by the light of a window; a teenager up late, blogging, e-mailing, or "chatting" as she sits in a dark room. Which image best characterizes life in the post-industrial west? Where we go from here may be a dark question.

·‿

This fall I made my last trip to the bramble near our house. The day before, a tractor had cleared ground, and when I walked to the patch the earth was scored with platting stakes. The bramble's days were numbered. Soon someone with a backhoe would excavate for the first of several houses; another would take a chain saw to the vines and douse the stubs with herbicide. By spring the only way back would be through memory, and memory would have to dig through asphalt and manicured lawns.

The electronic revolution reflects change, but hardly progress. A bramble adapts to changes in the weather, survives, and thrives as it can. It seeks water, sun, and minerals in the soil, doing its thing, season to season. While computers reveal a thirst for data and the need to control it, a blackberry patch offers freedom, abundance, and wanton sprawl—the life of the vegetable soul. The tangles are a nuisance to city planners, developers, lovers of asphalt and straight lines. A blackberry patch suggests not progress, but the interwoven density of life, its beauty and its risk. My memories of picking aren't stored in computer files, but in the air I breathe, on my tongue, and in the itch of my skin.

The bramble near our house is gone now. In September, I travel farther afield to find its kin, but a gulch or rail cut always obliges me. Blackberry picking isn't virtual reality, but the real, vital, thing. A machine, on the contrary, is designed to perform on its own. 129 Give it energy for start-up, and everything else falls into place, with, or without, regard for human input and interaction. However "interactive" we pretend they are, computers foster mechanical responses in us. Increasingly, we behave as they dictate, and indulge corresponding habits of body and mind.

Berry picking is a counter-behavior. It doesn't compute. So are backpacking, poetry writing, gardening, and meditation. If electronic culture survives and grows, these and similar disciplines, while always small pleasures, will become vital antidotes. Going after blackberries, letting them have at me, braces my courage, appetite, and pluck. It reconfirms that life is beautiful, seedy, and sweet. Berry picking fosters my quest to be whole, a word akin to *hale, heal, health, hallow,* and *holy.* Real people and places, like berry patches, are more powerful and intricate than any machine. I visited the patch near our house one more time, before it was bulldozed under. That day I paused in picking to commune with the dead. I tasted them in the bittersweet tang of blackberries.

Creel

To think is to forget.—Borges

"Moving sucks," my father frowned, and I knew he wasn't joking. For several hours we had lugged furniture and boxes into his driveway. Getting ready for a garage sale was work, but for him the event held more. Ten years of managing a duplex, tinkering with toilets, and haggling with tenants, had wrecked his knees and knuckles and tried his patience. And a bad heart and loneliness— my mother years dead—finally wore him down. The garage sale had him flummoxed. Should he part with the dresser they bought when they married in '37? Could he forgo his toolbox, the ancient screwdriver and ball-peen hammer—old-timers he no longer had use for?

Raised in Washington State by a cattle and sheep rancher driven to poverty in a swindle, my father nursed a miser's instinct. "Those garage-sale types want something for nothing," he grumped. He'd hold out for thirty bucks on the mattress, box springs, and frame; twenty for an old stuffed armchair. An oval mirror lined in fake gold filigree (his own find at a garage sale) and an end table with brass claw feet (a baroque art-deco hybrid his live-in girlfriend unloaded when she moved out) were marginal. And there were things my mother might have kept—copies of *Life, Look, The Saturday Evening Post;* scratchy vinyl recordings of Welk and Mantovani in tattered jackets; and assorted heirlooms shoved into the corners of memory. Eighty now, he had to scale down, but it hurt.

As I unpacked boxes, he carried out his old fishing creel. "This holds a story or two," he quipped, reaching for a stickum. The creel was pretty beaten up, but seeing it caught me short. When I was a boy, it hung in our basement storage room. It was woven of wicker, with a slot in the lid, and had a gamy smell. Dad scratched his chin. "Whadya think, five bucks?"

I hesitated.

"You want it, Bill?"

"Sure," I said as I reached for it.

For the next hour, I shuffled boxes, labeled stickums, and placed them on assorted items. Or my hands did. I was elsewhere: riding Dad's shoulders through fords too deep for me to wade; trailing him through dew-wet woods or watching a dry fly drift along a cut bank I thought his line could never have reached.

When he and my uncle Paul began fishing the rivers of west Montana, I was too young to wield a fly rod. I poked around in shallows; studied deer tracks in clay; or pondered the husks of larval insects that lay on rocks near the bank. But best of all were the trout in my father's creel. Sleek as melting ice, they lay staring up at me, as if I were some wondrous creature they were seeing for the first time.

My official chore on these trips, and the first I remember, was to line his creel with ferns. I cut fronds of bracken, wet them in the river, and placed them in the bed. They would keep trout cool in the heat, he said. As a kid, I took creels for granted. They were a fishermen's tool, vital as his rod or line, common as a sewing basket or lunch pail, though more handsome and durable.

That day at the garage sale, without realizing it, I accepted the burden of a legacy. The creel was like an old friend, but taking it troubled me. It held a weight I barely grasped, a mystery that had to do with my father and rivers. The wicker was stiff, but its weave was pliant. I felt like a kid who'd hooked an impossibly large trout, and a man still trying to land it.

·‿

When Paul died of leukemia at sixty, my father stopped fishing. By then I was a sulky, introverted teen who mistrusted his parents. Sometimes I'd wander down to the basement to see, but especially to smell, the creel. In the storage room, under the light of a dangling bulb, next to shelves lined with jars of plums, peaches, and pears; knickknacks; window blinds; and picture frames, all filmed with dust, I put my nose to the past. It was dry and musty, tainted with fern and willow, trout blood and scale. My father, too, was in that scent. It was an earthy smell that festered in the dark while everything else slept.

July 1955. Bitterroot River, Montana

This morning Dad hooks a big German Brown. It takes his fly at the end of a run of fast water and goes on a tear, zigzagging back and forth across the channel as line screams off his reel. The fish is strong and Dad scrambles along the bank, trying to land it. Holding a dip net, Uncle Paul waits in the shallows. Dad doesn't horse the fish, but lets it play itself out. It takes about half an hour. The trout is huge: its snout pokes from one end of the creel, its tail fin from the other. "It runs five pounds, if it runs an ounce," Paul grins. Dad hoists the brown out of the creel, runs a willow switch through its gills, lugs it to the car, and puts it in the cooler, where I get a better look. The big brown glistens—tan, green, gold, and spotted—like a gem pried from the river. It smells like a mix of fern and cod-liver oil.

The brown gets my blood running. I plunge into the river, slip, and nearly fall, casting frantically so my line tangles. While Dad fishes upstream, I slouch on the bank, head hung low. Suddenly he's beside me. "I'll give you a hand." He works at the knots in my leader. "Go loop by loop. Widen one, then another. If a knot is tight, use a hook to nudge it. But go easy—don't cut the nylon." He could have cut the leader and tied on a new one, but instead he works to salvage it. He seems to enjoy the labor. For him, knots hold a promise he wants to set free. At home, he can be short-tempered, but on the river he's in his element. After undoing the knots, he winks at me and says, "Carry on." 133

Near the end of his life, I moved my father to a care center near us. He was unhappy, often despondent. I would open his mail, read to him, take him to lunch or bring him cookies Cheryl had baked, but as months wore on he got more brittle and resistant. Knowing time was running out, he was afraid.

As adults my father and I were estranged. We never talked about it, but after he died the residue lingered. I smelled it in the closet of his apartment, where shirts, sweaters, and slacks hung in a slump now permanent. Maybe he never forgave me my adolescence, the "smart mouth" he tried to whip shut. Though we pretended to conceal it, we bristled at each other. One trusted the other to do the wrong thing. I was sarcastic and aloof; Dad carped under his breath.

The end came swiftly. It was a cold night in March. I had seen him early that evening, but just before midnight an attendant phoned, "You'd better hurry." I arrived at the care center just moments too late. Naked except for a diaper, Dad lay in bed, eyes glazed, mouth cocked wide. His sphincters had loosened and the room smelled of death. I thought I detected another scent, earthy and tainted, like leaves that had wintered under snow, exposed in spring raking. It was the smell of the creel and of rivers. Even the scent of water-repellent dressing—a wax called Mucilin, made of animal fat, he rubbed on his line and flies—came back. For a moment the creel's odor held the others, as if a coffin had opened to release an ancient perfume. It wasn't the smell of death, but life, earthy and sour, yet vital, as if time festered in it, wanting to bloom.

Then the smell of death returned—a soiled diaper on the bathroom floor; carpet cleaner and grime; body-must and sweat. I was alone with the body on the bed, and it belonged to a man I didn't know. The creel was far away, and everything lay wrecked, like a logjam that blocked a river's flow.

Honoring a request from my sister, who couldn't be with me, I fetched a bottle of baby lotion—Johnson & Johnson—from the bathroom and rubbed it into Dad's bony frame. Rigor hadn't set in yet. Though his body was scrawny—a mere one hundred fifteen pounds—his hands were limp as a baby's. The perfume of the lotion mingled with darker odors, like the love I wanted to feel but couldn't.

.➤

We play catch in the yard. The ball sails in an arc, whacking one mitt then the other, binding us together . . .

"Get to your room," he barks. There's a knot in my gut, nowhere to hide . . .

He stands behind me, hand on mine as I grip the fly rod. Swaying, we cast in tandem. I tense—he relaxed . . .

I toss the ball too high for him to catch it. He frowns and throws up his hands. "That's it, this game is over." He bristles and his face is ashen. "Good for nothing," he mutters and barrels past me toward the house . . .

When he slaps my shoulder, I beam. I have made the tenth-grade basketball team. "Outstanding," he chimes, "you've done me proud . . ."

Towering above me, his face twisted with rage, he jerks his belt from its loops . . .

As I swerve on my bright red birthday bike, he trots beside me, making sure I won't fall . . .

.➤

If wonder lives in the present and depends on forgetting, then memory is the enemy of wonder. We suspend what's routine or "over with" to get at the gold. After my father died, memory came often enough, at times passively, but in other times—I can think of no other word—*wondrously.*

At first, these visitations were troubling. In the past I had been defensive toward him. Afraid I wouldn't measure up, I bit my lip. A tall, slender man who got more bony as he aged, he took up more than his share of space. One Christmas in our dining room, my oldest son brushed past my father. Later, Bren told his mother, "It felt like I couldn't get by him, like he filled the whole room."

One morning a few days after he died, I was making coffee. I glanced at the walnut tree in the yard. Limbs like whips, it hadn't budded yet. A warm surge flooded my chest. I eased up on the grinder button and as the motor died, my father stood behind me. If I turned, he would be gone. He had suffered keenly, I felt. His illusions had burned away and left a searing clarity. He knew now who he was, or had been.

A few days later, my sister called to say he appeared to her in a dream. "I am not my body," he told her, as if he hoped she would embrace the change. Her dream reinforced my feeling that he was near. Did my grief prompt a sense of his release? Had I begun to let go of anger and fear? Strange as it seemed, I felt he was trying to help me.

⁓

My father kept no diary or journal. The few letters I have hold mostly factual advice—on taxes, inheritance, real estate—though even these, I now see, show his care. Most of the snapshots I have reveal a businessman's demeanor—Dad in double-breasted flannel, Dad in white shirt with starched collar. Only a few fishing shots find him at ease, the man the child in me admires. In the months after his death, stories he told came in a flood. At odd hours, I repeated the stories aloud to myself until I heard his voice in mine. Sometimes he spoke in the present tense.

June 1918

When I was ten my father took me into the Blue Mountains of eastern Oregon where he herded sheep. After losing the family ranch in a swindle, he took odd jobs to support us. He had been a herder years before, in the 1880s, when he first came west. As we trail the flock through a meadow, Frenchie, our cook, scolds the mule pulling the chuck wagon. It's late afternoon. My father waves at Frenchie to stop, and the dingoes, Shep and Ernie, circle the flock until the sheep lie down. "William, go fetch supper," my father hollers, and I ride in search of a creek we passed a mile or so back.

When I get there, I tie my pony's reins on a pine bough and carry my rucksack to the bank. With a jackknife I cut a willow switch, notch the tip, tie on a length of cotton twine, and cinch a safety pin to the end. The creek is thick with brook trout. They smack the safety pin like crazy—I don't even need bait. At dusk I pack a mess into the rucksack, dip it in the creek, and ride back to camp as sun sinks into the pines. I know this will be one of the happiest days of my life.

·

When my father sold the duplex, I forgot about the creel. Several weeks after he died, it came knocking. I hadn't seen it in months, or was it years? After the garage sale, I had stored it our basement, but rummaging the shelves and searching the toolshed outside brought no luck. Had I given it to Bren, our oldest son, now a fisherman himself? A phone call set me straight. What could I have done with it? How could I have been so careless? I remembered the creel resting beside paint cans and tools, but even that image had grown dim. It was an emblem of my anger and regret, and a link to the past and to my father.

In his last months Dad grew thin and frail. Once, hunched at his desk, checkbook open and pen in hand, he couldn't muster a scrawl. His checkbook meant everything to him. It epitomized his anxiety about money, his urge to keep things neat and predictable. If I obsessed over the creel, he obsessed over his checkbook. It held a record of what mattered most. That day when I wrote the check for him, he thanked me, grimly. He may have sensed what lay ahead. A week after he died, as I sorted his things, I found the checkbook again. It had his smell in it.

137

In my father's struggle, I saw the specter of my own aging. There was Alzheimer's (would I become one of the now over five million?); assisted living (corporately financed dormitories designed for profit, several of which Dad had lived in, unhappily); and the inevitable, apocalyptic shrinking of options—one's bodily health, domicile, and economic means. What's more, Cheryl and I would soon retire, relocate, and begin a new phase of our life together.

The creel, or its memory, evoked a past I wanted back, but fumbled to find. Often, my identity seemed a sham and the past as ephemeral as it was troubling. I had opened the creel and found an abyss. I tried sketching the creel, but there was much I had forgotten. How wide was the sewn leather frame? Was the slot you dropped a trout through framed with leather too? My first attempt looked like a crude impression of a toolbox. I ransacked our closet for photographs with no luck. Did I recall rib work on the creel's lid—large strips of wicker in the warp and slender strands in the woof? That would account for the ribbed feel I remembered. I sketched the band of leather sewn across the lid, the buckle on the front below it—was it tin or steel? I drew the leather loop attached to the back for hanging, what creel-makers call the "iris." I floundered hopelessly.

Still, the creel wouldn't let go. White space wanted to be filled. I scrawled mere hints: wicker dark with blood; trout whose skin air had brushed to ruin; a withered shroud of fern. It was no longer the creel I drew, but what it carried, and what it carried welled inside me, as if the lid flipped open and the best things in my life spilled out. Then my father tapped my shoulder, as if I were the trout he was trying to catch.

My father took great care as a fisherman. He gutted a trout with patience and precision, as if he performed a rite. With a jackknife, he'd slit a cutthroat's belly from the vent to the gills, press his left thumb through its lower jaw, and with his right thumb and forefinger grip the upper viscera and rip down hard, making

138

a sound like fabric being torn. The innards looked like a tangled mesh of jellyfish and smelled like bacon grease and manure. Inside us tubes, sacs, bubbles, knots, flukes, and cords throbbed, wriggled, and sucked. If flesh was woven, strands of mind and heart were the hardest to see.

Once hiking along the Spokane River as a boy, I spotted a creel resting on the bottom near shore. The current was strong and too deep for me to wade, so I stood and stared. The creel had been in the river awhile. It bore a fleece of algae and weeds stuck in the wicker swayed like muskrat tails. The river carried the creel, and the creel the river. It showed me you could hold things you couldn't see. I wondered if things I couldn't see held me. A lifetime later, thinking of that day, I see my father standing on the far bank. Rod in hand, creel slung from his shoulder, he waves and is gone.

·ᴗ

In the Northwest, the best-known creel-maker when my father was growing up was the George Lawrence Company of Portland, maker of saddlery and harnesses. Catering to a Western audience, Lawrence framed his creels with leather, making them more durable for fishermen of backcountry rivers, who bushwhacked rough terrain. The first leather-worked creel in the Lawrence catalogue appeared in 1923, when my father was fifteen. Staring at a picture of it, I heard his voice again. Now he spoke from memory.

> *I grew up a bait fisherman, like other boys I knew. In those days Mill Creek ran free through the center of town. Unless you count sandbags and backaches, there was no flood control to speak of then. Now the creek is harnessed in a concrete sluice box, but in those days it was lined with cottonwoods and willows.*
>
> *One July—it was hot as blazes—no one could catch anything with worms or salmon eggs. The trout were sluggish, not hungry, or else hungry for something else. At the Rexall soda fountain, I complained to a friend about it, and the druggist—what was his name,*

*Abernathy, Abercrombie?—overheard me and offered the loan of his
fly rod. "Cast lightly," he said. "Keep the tip of the rod at eye level.
Let your line drift but keep it taut. Make sure the fly is floating—if it
disappears jerk the rod hard to set the hook. Play the fish, don't horse
it."*

*The next morning boys and a few dads were fishing with no luck.
I tied on a fly—a gray-hackle peacock, like Aber-whatever had
recommended—and started casting. I was sloppy at first, but when
I got the hang of it, my fly started floating. I was the only one who
caught fish on that stretch, and believe me, I got attention. Fly-fishing
was a novelty then, a British sport mostly, but with Aber-whatever's
help, I made inroads. I saw more guys with fly rods after that.*

As I sorted my father's things, made funeral arrangements, and
contacted relatives, our estrangement cut deep. We hadn't had
the courage to face it. When I turned fifty, I dropped the initial,
Jr., from my name. I told myself it was for simplicity's sake, but I
begrudged him. He knew it, and begrudged me, but, as always,
neither of us brought it up.

I wanted to lick my wounds, but it was healing that mattered.
As hard as I fought it, I needed to celebrate my father's life. Be ye
fishers of men, I had been taught as a child. Now I was fishing for
my father, not to save him, not even to know him—an impossible
task, I now saw—but to plumb the nature of memory as a way to
him and back. To embrace who he was, and let go.

No slipshod, fly-by-night sportsman, Dad prepared carefully
for a fishing trip. Like a jeweler hunkered over a watch, he sat
140 at a washroom table to inspect his fly rod, squinting down the
lengths for cracks in the lacquer or guides that were missing,
broken, or snapped. Bent to a small work lamp, next to scissors,
thread, lacquer, and a tiny brush, he scraped, daubed, wound, and
taped. His work held the integrity of art. Doing what he loved
required skill and sacrifice. Years later Dickinson's lines would

remind me—"Power is only pain / stranded through discipline." It was fishing that he loved. To do it, and do it well, he honored his tools. This increased his chances not only for catching trout, but for finding beauty and grace. When he finished his repairs, he stood and shook the rod lightly. It wagged like a dog's tail, not sideways but vertically, and I felt the tug of a river.

⌣

Maybe the real blessing isn't memory but forgetting. If we remembered everything, the inability to forget would cripple us. Like Borges's character, Funes, in "Funes, the Memorious," we would remember every detail of our lives, but be unable to distinguish the trivial from the essential. Facing a choice, we'd be paralyzed.

Can forgetting free memory to go deeper? On one level, I was a boy looking for his father. On another, I probed the source of sentience itself, my coming of age in the natural world. Maybe the creel epitomized the weave of Earth's own intelligence, stress lines in rock, sap lines in trees, the meandering veins of rivers. Maybe if I quit trying, or needing, to remember, the past would let go. Or come back more clearly.

The creel's odor went deep. I probed the science of smell, but for the most part, came up empty. Smell is the sensory receptor hardest to explain. Some chemists call it "the last mystery of the senses." Probing molecular structures and neurological systems has offered explanations of sight, taste, hearing, and touch, but not smell. I tried to imagine odor molecules that could interpenetrate with receptor proteins in my nostrils; how these proteins manage to tunnel into electrons. In effect, a kind of sensory, and extrasensory, dance occurred in my nose, where the boundaries between matter and spirit blurred. But I floundered. What did any of this have to do with my father or the creel? What lingered in that earthy, unforgettable, smell?

When I was a boy, Dad's own smell seemed the most powerful thing about him. His sour, male fetor, as much as what he said or

141

did, let me know him. And then, like a lightning bolt, memory shot back its question. Did the intimacy of scent mean more to me because I had *not* known intimacy of other kinds, the unconditional love every child craves? Had I loved rivers because *they* took me in?

As a boy I learned from woods and rivers because I was part of them. I was no critic or calculator. My curiosity was instinctual, like a bear sniffing honey or a woodpecker hacking bark. The shape, color, and position of a rock in the river made it beg to be pried up and looked under. It became the form of my emotion discovering itself.

Years later, when I read Edith Cobb's *The Ecology of Imagination in Childhood*, I was primed. As a child starts exploring the world, she explains, curiosity and the desire for fulfillment merge. Our nervous systems, the contours of our awareness, are wired for apprehending textures, shapes and colors, the grainy feel of things. I thought of willows that both hide and reveal what's around a river bend, when the play of limbs and light verge not on closure, but a sense of what's about to be. Cobb calls this way of knowing "wonder." For her, it's the distinctive trait of childhood, but also the foundation of both logic and creativity.

The creel holds the river my father wades through. A tiny speck at the end of his leader drifts in and out of eyeshot. He's after trout, but it feels like the whole river, its trees and sunlight, its rocky bed and current, rises to meet him, as if time, place, and his effort have called them forth. And I'm the boy who is there to see it. Because of my father I'm part of it too.

Maybe losing the creel wasn't so bad after all. Now I can retrieve it in other ways. One life, however partial in the living, however poorly understood, reflects the life of us all. A few days before my father died, I hugged him. It didn't come naturally. Before leaving his apartment, as he rose feebly from his chair, I swallowed hard, put my arms around him, and squeezed. He squeezed back, stiff and resistant as always. When I said, "I love you," he wheezed the same to me—words I'd never heard from him before.

There's a fine line between forgetting and letting go, a fly line perhaps, that as it unravels creates an arc between air and water, the present and the past, and which as it lands on the river holds life suspended for a second, when everything waits to mesh, as if the current and the line unfolding into it are themselves weaving, and woven into, a larger pattern. The creel has come to hold more. The latest addition is a handful of Dad's ashes I tossed into an Idaho river a year ago. They didn't dissolve, but lay stranded on the sandy bottom, like spackle the current laid down.

·＿

A voice echoes down the stairwell, "Billy, rise and shine." I wake as my father calls me. It's three a.m. Pitch dark. A cold June morning . . .

With a start I remember we're going fishing. I stretch, yawn, hurry into my clothes, and clamber upstairs to the kitchen. Dad and Paul are scarfing down bacon, eggs, and toast. Mom wears a pink bathrobe, hair sprouting pin curlers as she fusses over the stove. The smell of hot grease, rich coffee, the day just beginning . . .

On newspaper spread on the dining-room floor, lines and leaders are laid out to dry. The day before, my father soaked them in tins of water, so they wouldn't kink or knot when he fished. When I stare at the loops, the river eddies back . . .

No traffic as we leave town. The city shrouded in fog. A milk truck waits at a stoplight, "Carnation" stenciled on its side, the driver impossible to see . . .

Dad casts toward the far bank, and from where I stand, I can see his fly. It drifts through a seam of light and shadow. For a second, I can see—no—feel time in my bones, what was, is, and shall be, all coming together. A glint of silver darts through the water—a trout otherwise invisible, ever about to be . . .

As my father drives home in the dark, I lie in the backseat and glance through the window at the moon. When I lift my hand, trout scale glitters on my fingers. I touch, and am touched by, stars . . .

143

The Circle of Time

"Hi, bug," Noah chirps. The crane fly shudders, then goes still. We're on the sofa, our backs to the room, looking out the window. I kneel—Noah stands. When I draw up the shade, he discovers the insect posed upright on the sill, legs and wings intact, as if it rests before taking flight.

In the parking lot in front of Suzanne's apartment, maple samaras toggle down to the asphalt. Wind frisks the tree near her window, but Noah isn't watching that. Instead, he's fascinated by his new friend. And cautious. He wants to touch the fly, but insists that I do it first, tugging my index finger until I tap the insect lightly.

"Careful, we don't want to break your bug."

"No break bug. Hi, bug."

The crane fly must have flown in when the door was open on a sunny day a few weeks ago. When it lodged behind the blinds and was unable to escape, it got scorched. Legs spindly, all six still intact, it looks like an oversized mosquito, and having been thoroughly bleached, is about the same color.

"The bug can't fly because it's dead."

I congratulate myself for speaking nonsense to a three-year-old. In any case, Noah proves me wrong. He takes a breath, puffs at the crane fly, and sends it tumbling a foot or so along the sill. He doesn't repeat the word *dead*, which he may not, probably hasn't, heard before. Instead he grins and blows again. "Bug fwy!" he delights.

The crane fly tumbles again and this time comes apart. Noah doesn't seem troubled by this, only glances about trying locate the pieces. I retrieve a wing that fell to the heat register, but by now he has lost interest.

"Play baskaball 'gain?"

Vertical moments are rare. Sometimes, in a flash, an experience cuts through, or into, time. We slow down, our pores open, and life breathes. Attention gets keener, feeling verges on reflection, and for moment, things vibrate at a higher pitch. These can be times of pain, joy, grief, or a mingling of all three. I felt that way during the births of each of our children. It was as if, to revive an old phrase, "the glory of the heavens had opened" and raised me up or come down into my arms as a slick, pink, puling, helpless little being I knew was an angel.

Once, before the crane fly came apart, Noah noticed how still it was and exclaimed, "Znot movin." To be alive is to move, and to perceive motion. But for Noah, something that doesn't move, and never will again, can be equally alive. He saw the fly lay still, then breathed it the breath of life. But even when it didn't move, he spoke to it as a living being.

We often hear that a child's perception is egocentric or self-centered, but neither term will quite do. The young child has no ego or self to be centered on. Instead, the world is a field of rich and varied impressions the child is part of. The mix is largely undifferentiated. What the child does have is a gradually dawning awareness of his or her involvement, or in-dwelling connection with, what eventually becomes the "outer" world. The idea of a separate ego is an adult projection, not a young child's experience. The child seems egocentric because he or she, in effect, *is* the world. Only later in childhood, when the ego begins to form, does the child feel apart from it.

The psychologist Edith Cobb calls this early relationship "a wordless dialectic between self and world," with the stress on "dialectic." She argues that a child experiences the natural world as a cosmos, or unified whole, and does so passionately, though not erotically, on the perceptual level. The child senses his or her own "psycho-physical" growth as a "continuity of nature's behavior." She found a direct statement of it in a poem of Whitman's:

145

There was a child went forth every day,
And the first object he looked upon, that object he became,
And that object became part of him for the day or a certain part of the
*   day,*
Or for many years or stretching cycles of years.

Participation plays into the child's knowing in ways we hardly grasp. Even before he toddled, Noah felt connected to everything. There was no sharp boundary between self and other, animate and inanimate. "Need hug?" he would ask a fence post or rock wall. Sometimes he behaved this way to something one of us had pointed to, but often not. It could be the branch of a tree I lifted him to touch—like the cherry in our former front yard—or a mailbox, or the neighbor's dog. Last week when he toddled around a parked car, he hugged a tire and said, "Hi, tire." It could be, as behaviorists argue, that Noah transfers his mother's hugs to "inert" things; but it could also be, as Cobb and others suggest, that he experiences the world differently than adults do. Noah treats tires and concrete with the same affection he gives us, all the more remarkable when we consider that a tire won't hug back. It's as if his feeling and seeing cancel out, or re-form, what rational adults would say isn't, and can't be, alive; as if Noah senses the inner form of things as living presences akin to his own.

For most adults in western, industrial culture, it takes a self-willed act of imagining to give a car a hug and mean it, car fanatics aside. We call this "personifying" and consider it a form of metaphoric behavior. But haven't most of us experienced such contact, prior to reflection? A mechanical friend of mine talks to his cars, pats and pets them. He knows how to fix them, too, and this can be very deliberate, calculative work; but the bottom line is—he loves them.

Many children, and some adults, feel this way about plants, animals, water, or clouds. For adults, steel, concrete, and rubber are tougher, but with the help of advanced physics and a dash of creative invention, we can approach them too, not by entering a scientific laboratory, but by a willed act of imagination. Noah's high chair looks like a stationary object because my eyes aren't powerful enough to observe atomic waves and particles churning inside it. On the other hand, through imagination, I can, to some extent, envision this process occurring.

I may be going out on a limb, but I believe it will hold. I'm not suggesting that we blindly repudiate "facts," but that we call into question the nature of facts and how we experience them. I believe this process is historically determined, and so subject to change, but our current climate of opinion, still shaped by Newtonian science and the image of the world as a machine (via the industrial revolution), is prone to ignore it.

Instead of asserting this as an idea, however, I want to call attention to the experience *behind* the idea. Observing how my three-year-old grandson approaches the world has been my starting point. As long as the limb holds, I want to explore what I have seen, and how this, in turn, has affected my thinking. The now habitual notion that the phenomenal world exists apart from human consciousness is at the root of the problem. But if, by observing and questioning, by looking at our own behavior, we're able to call that felt, yet unprovable, premise into question, fresh possibilities arise. Right now, I ask myself: if I exert a measure of will and reflection, can I re-envision what for Noah is direct, spontaneous experience?

Something else happened when he said "hi" to the crane fly. While the maple samaras were falling, Noah zeroed in on one and said, "Izza bug. Iz fwying." So, again, he brought the crane fly back to life. Metaphor came naturally. When a garbage truck 147 pulled up to the apartment complex and its steel pincers lifted a dumpster, Noah mimicked it aloud, "Up down, up down," and the big yellow truck was surely alive. The man in middle age and the grandchild just coming on may experience life differently, but we shared the crane fly's flight. Noah does it spontaneously, through unconscious participation. I do it by a kind of second sight, not with theories or doctrines, but as imagined re-seeing, what the poet Rilke, recalling a dog he observed, called "in-seeing":

> *to let yourself precisely into the dog's center, the point from which it begins to be a dog, the place where God, as it were, would have sat down for a moment when the dog was finished, in order to watch it during its first embarrassments and inspirations and to nod that it was good, that nothing was lacking, that it couldn't have been better made.*

Or as Rilke suggested elsewhere, God wants to know himself in us and does so when we know ourselves in other parts of the creation.

Cheryl's mother is nearing the end of life. She is increasingly frail, wheezes asthmatically when she exerts, and her skin has become translucent, as if it now consists as much of light as of tissue. Cheryl worries about her, and recently we talked about our own aging and the changes it would bring. I had been thinking about this when Noah saw the crane fly. In that moment, the unseen or immaterial part of being alive suggested a simple truth: for Noah there is no death.

One can't be a child again. But one can—indeed, must, if we are to sustain the earth and ourselves—live in touch with the inside or invisible part of what's "out there." This is no blithe fantasy. It does not mean we become blind to the material world, or that we will avert grief or ruin. I will lose Cheryl one day, or she me, and I shudder to think it. I can't think it. I avert my eyes. We have grown together in ways largely interior, unseen by ordinary eyes, including our own. Ways akin to Noah's seeing, in which a feeling for the immaterial energies around and within us are felt so keenly we partly "see" them in the other. And in the times we are capable of that, there is no death, only the life of the present moment.

That people share a perceivable world at all is possible only because consciousness and phenomena conjoin at a subliminal level of awareness. Like it or not, we humans, like everything else, are woven into the world's fabric, from respiration, circulation, metabolism, on up to, and possibly through, consciousness itself. A child revels in mud and stamps the puddle. A gardener feels kin to the earth she turns with a spade. But such tangible contact and the feeling it inspires now seem exceptions to the general rule. Over the past few centuries, having evolved into the great "cut off," consciousness, collectively speaking, has severed itself from phenomena. Things go on, as we say, "without us," and we look at the world from indoors, sealed by the walls of our skin, and the lonely restlessness inside.

If Pascal's oft-quoted proverb is true—"all the unhappiness of men arises from a single fact, that they cannot stay quietly in their own chamber"—it may be because we experience that self as cut off, unserved, cast back on its own, undernourished resources. We're slaves to an ever speeded up, ever shifting "outness" spawned by rampant development, ads, and a cancerous explosion of information. There's a maggot in our heads. Our mass distraction is consuming. The commerce and entertainment industries pander to a Coke-machine mentality that craves cheap gratification and the quick fix. We are the culture of salad shooters, big-screen TVs, and mood-altering drugs. Each day, in magazines, newspapers, and movies, on TV, radio, cell phones, computers, billboards, and marquees, we are bombarded with ads, which for many, now constitute perhaps the single most familiar reality.

But there are signs that the paradigm is crumbling. The roots of consumer capitalism, which have for so long fed on the poisons of greed and extraction, are withering. In spite of mainstream power and money, which still rule, we're getting serious about renewable *149* energy, not just materially, but spiritually. The next time you see small children playing, stop and observe closely. What can they teach you? To probe the nature of consciousness, cultivate art. What would it mean to take Blake's affirmation seriously, as practice, if only for an hour, or a day?

To see a World in a Grain of Sand
And a Heaven in a Wild Flower,
Hold Infinity in the palm of your hand
And Eternity in an Hour.

ᐧᐧᐧ

A few weeks ago we had a big laugh. Noah loves going to the park to swing and slide. He insists on it and is sad when he can't. But when he got a throat infection, started an antibiotic, and stayed home from preschool, the park was out of the question. He became even more insistent. "Go park? Go park, Nana?" This time Cheryl was ready for him. She knelt, looked into his eyes, and spoke firmly, "Why can't Noah go to the park? One: it's cold outside. Two: Noah's sick." Then she got Noah to repeat. "Noah can't go park. One: code owside. Two: Noah sick." When Suzanne got home from work, we all said it and laughed together. Noah laughed the hardest.

He had just started counting. He loved the repetition in it, as he did in the songs we sang, and seemed to delight in rhythm—bouncing, nodding, clapping, dancing. Often, he seemed wholly immersed in things. When Noah counted caterpillars in his caterpillar book, he always pointed and touched. He would grab our fingers so we could touch too, the way he did with the crane fly. When he repeated aloud the little mantra about the park, he must have felt a similar pleasure, and suddenly his not going to the park didn't matter. He had found a new connection, in words, voice, and rhythm, which were a form of play themselves. When we laughed, the crane fly buzzed behind my eyes.

150   If we spent less time thinking *about* the world—as external data—and more time thinking *into* it—as an intricate and interconnected dance of matter and mind—we'd realize that adults can participate too. Explaining this, though perhaps abstract at first, is a means to experiencing it. If the heart follows the head, we must think about thinking. That we experience a world of inert

things, apart from us, with no correlative in our consciousness, is a habit of recent history, one with certain consequences. But it's also a habit that, with practice, we can break.

⤙

A few months back, on a chilly spring morning, Cheryl and I drove into the Blue Mountains of southeast Washington. We hiked up a tree-lined canyon along a creek. In an open stretch, I stopped to scan a far slope with field glasses. When Cheryl walked a few yards ahead, she startled an animal on a ridge above the trail. Tawny, quick, low to the ground, it bounded off before she got a good look. I never saw it, only heard the clack of loose rock when the critter, whatever it was, leapt to run.

It moved alone, and its body was long and lean. Probably not a deer. Cheryl felt it was a cougar and she was shaken. When I quizzed her, she gave me the inside scoop.

"I felt it before I saw it. A space opened in the top of my head and the lion ran through. I'm not just material, you know."

"You're not dense, either."

"Am I subtle matter?"

"Yup. You've been cougared, mother."

From then on we glanced at the breaks to see if we were being followed. Did Cheryl "in-see" a mountain lion, the way Rilke did a dog? Not exactly—she didn't have much time. But whatever happened, she was immersed in it, part of a larger, subtler field of occurrence, something she sensed before she thought *about* it. Later, I recalled Noah finger painting. He sits on his picture as he paints and slaps the color all around, not just on butcher paper, but all over himself. Paint is part of him, and vice versa. He becomes paint and paint paints him. Crazy, right? But when I try to get inside of what I see, that's how it comes out. He participates his painting, swims and wallows in it. He's happy, focused, and gleefully present all at once. He doesn't think about it—he *is* it.

151

I come back to the crane fly. What I first saw as a thing, Noah saw as an image. Owen Barfield explains the difference this way: "an image presents itself as an exterior expressing or implying an interior, whereas a thing does not." Noah gave the crane fly his heart. I started with my head, and taking his cue, worked backwards.

The earth is in peril because we see it, and treat it, as a thing. Despite its expertise and achievement, science has spawned an isolative frame of mind. In freeing us from traditional images of and relationships to the cosmos, it bequeathed us a world of "things," the material equivalents of unchanging natural laws understood mechanically. The modern scientific revolution was a glorious and necessary triumph, but we're still in a tailspin about the results. Our tinkering, now down to proton splitting, only seems to atomize us further. Physicists propose ever more intricate mathematical models of how it all came about and where it might be going, but the question of our experience—what consciousness is, how it came about, and how we might use it to heal ourselves and our world—is lost in a maze of abstraction. Understanding remains esoteric, always in need of translating. Can the oscillating super-strings and implicate orders physicists conjure with numbers be found in paintings, stories and poems, or in the dreams that so move and puzzle us?

The style of consciousness from which science grew and which it still reinforces has hardened into habit. I'll be the first to praise science and technology—for antibiotics, heart valves, fiber optics, and a vast array of life-enhancing projects and gadgets, as well as for the miracles of molecular biology and advanced physics. But the problem runs deeper. With certain exceptions in physics, scientific discovery and research still focus primarily on discrete, isolated parts of a larger and mysterious whole. If we don't perceive and respect this whole in the long run—if we don't, that is, train ourselves to *experience* it from within—the parts won't matter. As we continue tinkering with the "outside" of nature, depleting its resources and obsessing with external "fixes," we continue to become more like machines ourselves, re-creating the Earth in our own image.

The inner world too is at risk. Darwin's breakthrough, while profound, was also tragic. He left out one vital component—consciousness—whose evolution, were it granted equal rank along with matter (instead of viewed as some inexplicable spin-off) would turn both science and religion, including the simplistic literalism of "creation by design," on their heads.

It matters how we see, but also how we don't, as Emerson knew: "The ruin that we see in nature is in our own eye." What we *fail* to perceive is as important as what we do perceive. The crane fly reminded me. Ideas *about* things are less to the point than *how* we experience things. In classical Greek, the word for idea, *idein*, means "to see." If the heart follows the head, and I believe it does, then thinking about how we see is more vital now then ever. To realize that earlier cultures had not just different ideas than we do, but actually *saw* a different world, is to realize dynamic change is inherent in the development of consciousness, as it is in flora, fauna, and geologic formations. With the fate of the earth in the offing, it matters supremely where we go from here. To most the idea that consciousness evolves is a shocking surprise. To think that consciousness may, after all, be more than a latter-day reflex of chemistry is more shocking still.

When Noah said "bug," he meant something different than I do. His "meaning" included form, shape, and common association, like mine, and did not include technical knowledge or familiarity. But it also included an immediate identification, a felt, if unconscious, sense that the crane fly and he were alive in similar ways. On this count, the notion that a child's awareness parallels that of earlier humanity is worth pondering.

153

Many pre-literate cultures would have viewed Noah's crane-fly episode as an encounter with divinity. So would have people in the European Middle Ages. For the ancient Egyptians, the sun was a god. For the Romans, wind was *spiritus*, the all-informing breath. To label such thinking as "animism" presumes a de-animated nature minds like our own have invented, or inherited as habit. These early cultures, so the thinking goes, project their own, wholly interior, feelings or beliefs onto inert phenomena that operate by what we understand as "natural" laws. But what if early people had no wholly interior experience of the world? What if they understood nature by different "laws" than we do, laws more akin to mythology than mathematics?

The word *phenomenon* is a case in point. For Greeks like Plato, *phainomenon* meant a "showing or shining forth," akin to the power of light, and suggested that material things have an expressive life we share. In truth, *we* live in, and perceive, a different world than earlier cultures did. What we view as quaint errors may arise from qualitatively different minds, and hence, different phenomena, all together.

Noah's experience of a bug, his sense of the word, has historical antecedents. Consider how the meanings of words change over time. In our calendar, names of months and days once honored rulers, rites, gods, and goddesses—April for Aphrodite, Monday the moon, Thursday Thor, and so on. That the word *genius* once meant "tutelary spirit," that *panic* once referred to animals possessed by a god, and *psyche* to "soul," "moth," and "butterfly," is to realize that, over time, consciousness has moved indoors. A process of internalization has drained meaning from the outer appearances and sucked it into our interior selves. It's as if life were drawn out of the sea and sequestered on a walled island where it remains shipwrecked, imprisoned, and out of touch with the world that once nurtured and sustained it. For detailed illustration, I refer the reader to the work of Owen Barfield, who provides historical and theoretical foundations for the study of meaning, metaphor, and consciousness.

We can't go back. But we can help direct how we go on. Metaphor is not just a literary device but a "meaning-making"

154

power, a component of perception itself. Before there was glass, a *window* was the "wind's eye." Whoever understood the word that way was not cut off from phenomena, not just looking *at* them, but part of them, built into their significant life breath. When that person looked through a window, God—as wind–spirit—breathed behind her eyes. If a *daisy* is a flower, it is also, etymologically, the "day's eye," an epitome of life-informing fire.

To respect and appreciate such histories fully would be to provide a new basis for scientific understanding. We would work not just from the head down, and from matter out, but from the ground, and the body, up. To understand matter would also be to understand spirit. Instead of tinkering with the outside of nature, we could begin apprehending and possibly changing it, and ourselves, from within, as Goethe urged nearly two centuries ago.

If the young science of ecology—the "study of home"—is ever to help, it must turn from mere tinkering to matters of spirit. Efforts at legislation, environmental cleanup, recycling, and climate change will be meaningless otherwise. When science becomes a bridge to spirit, when we understand the laws of nature are laws of the mind, healing may begin. True, we need lab rats, cyclotrons, and calculative geniuses, but we need imagination more. Doing research or winning government contracts will matter only when they come from *contact*, a relation both genuine and deep.

Imagine a mathematician for whom pure numbers spin like Plato's spheres; a physicist whose equation doesn't stop with the dry-erase marker but approaches cosmic bliss; a biologist who envisions cellular infrastructure when she admires a Pollock print. In fact, we already have such visionaries, but their insights—the way they actually see—don't get into mainstream research or textbooks and trickle down to the rest of us. Instead, we continue to treat the world as if it were a machine and in turn, we, and the world, become more like one.

Noah's meeting with the crane fly reminded me I'm not yet a machine. Time doesn't run in a straight line. If you're religious, the dead don't have to wait until the end of days to live again. If you're scientific, a systematic use of imagination can vivify the unseen until it becomes a way of knowing. How did that Joni Mitchell tune go—we can't return, we can only look behind from where we came and go round and round and round in the circle game?

A child begins the world again, and parents and grandparents celebrate that joy. Noah is teaching us how it's so. In Hebrew his name means "rest," "peace," or "comforter." It may look to a world restored after terrifying destruction, and the peace that comes from the work that makes it so.

The other day when Noah stayed with us, it rained. Afterwards we all went outside to see a rainbow. It was Ishtar's jeweled necklace before it was Yahweh's bow; and it was the natural wonder honored in our grandchild's name. But at the time I didn't have to recall any of that. In his own way, Noah already knew. He looked at the sky, pointed, and smiled. He saw where the arc began, then ran around the house to see where it came down. The circle was whole. We saw its promise in his eyes.

Acknowledgments

My thanks to the following books, periodicals, and their editors, for publishing earlier versions of these essays:

"Brute Neighbors," *Black Canyon Quarterly* (Fall 2002), pp. 30-37.

"Hiking the Selway at Night," in *Written on Water: Essays on Idaho Rivers*, Ed. Mary Blew, University of Idaho Press (2001), pp. 93-104.

"The Patience of Hawks," in *Borne on Air: Essays by Idaho Writers*, Ed. Mary Blew and Phil Druker, Eastern Washington University Press (2009), pp. 85-96.

"Stories We Are, Stories We Become," formerly "Clearwater Journal," in *Holding Common Ground: The Individual and Public Lands in the American West*, ed. P. Lindholdt and D. Knowles, Eastern Washington University Press (2005), pp. 109-113.

"Risking the West," *Petroglyph* 10 (1998), pp. 12-16.

"The Circle of Time," formerly "Millennium Song," in *Connections* (Winter 2000), pp. 23-25.

"Warmed Twice," in *Forged in Fire: Essays by Idaho Writers*, Ed. Mary Blew and Phil Druker, University of Oklahoma Press (2005), pp. 159-169.

William Stafford, "Ask Me" from *The Way It Is: New and Selected Poems*. Copyright © 1977 1998 by William Stafford and the Estate of William Stafford. Reprinted with the permission of Graywolf Press, Minneapolis, Minnesota, www.graywolfpress.org.

⌣

I'm grateful to those who introduced me to Idaho, its people, history, creatures, and places: Horace Axtell, Bert Bowler, Morton Brigham, Cort Conley, Steve Evans, Pam and Craig Gehrke, Eileen and Archie George, Allen Marshall, Hugh Nichols, Jim Seamons, Erica Starr, and Mary Waters; and to those who read and commented on early drafts of this book: Mary Blew, M.K. Browning, Cort Conley, Phil Druker, Okey Goode, James Hepworth, Gary Holthaus, and Peter Matthiessen.

Thanks to Micki Reaman of Oregon State University Press for her kind and thorough editorial assistance.

I owe special thanks to my wife, Cheryl Johnson, whose grace, humor, and wisdom have sustained me.

Notes and Comments

Walking the Bridge Rail

p. 11. Paul Shepard. "A Post-historic Primitivism," in *The Wilderness Condition*, Max Oelschlaeger, editor (Washington, D.C.: Island Press, 1992), 46.

p. 12. Gary Holthaus. *Learning Native Wisdom* (Lexington: University of Kentucky, 2008), 185.

p. 12. Rainier Maria Rilke. "Duino Elegies." Number 4. Lines 16-18. *The Selected Poetry of Rainier Maria Rilke*, Stephen Mitchell, editor and translator (New York: Vintage, 1989), 169.

p. 12. E. O. Wilson. *The Diversity of Life* (New York: Norton, 1992), 350.

p. 12. Ralph Waldo Emerson. "Nature," in *Selections from Ralph Waldo Emerson*, Stephen Whicher, editor (Boston: Houghton-Mifflin, 1960), 55.

Risking the West

p. 23. Meriwether Lewis and William Clark. *The Journals of Lewis and Clark*. Frank Bergon, editor (New York: Penguin, 1989).

Brute Neighbors

p. 31. John Fowles. *The Tree* (Boston: Little Brown, 1979), cited in *The Norton Anthology of Nature Writing*. R. Finch & J. Elder, editors (New York: Norton, 1990), 669.

p. 34. Henry David Thoreau. The Maine Woods (1863). *Walden and Other Other Writings*. W. Howarth, editor (New York: Random House, 1981), 52-53.

p. 36. Paul Shepard. *Thinking Animals* (Athens: University of Georgia, 1998).

p. 36. Galway Kinnell. "On the Oregon Coast" in *The Past* (Boston: Houghton Mifflin, 1985), 36.

p. 36. Henry David Thoreau. *The Variorum Walden* (New York: Twayne, 1962), 124.

Stories We Are, Stories We Become

p. 42. Mary Waters was a traditional Nez Perce storyteller who gained the respect of the local tribal community. She died a few years after we heard her tell the tale of Coyote and Swallowing Monster.

The Floating World
p. 58. Theodore Roethke. "The Waking," in *The Collected Poems of Theodore Roethke* (New York: Anchor, 1975), 104.
p. 61. Saint Augustine. *Confessions.* Trans. R. S. Pine-Coffin. (Baltimore: Penguin, 1961), Bk. IX, sec. 8, 194.

Warmed Twice
p. 64. Henry David Thoreau. The Maine Woods (1863). *Walden and Other Other Writings.* W. Howarth, editor (New York: Random House, 1981), 210.
p. 71. *James* 6-10 (Revised Standard Version)
p. 71. Emily Dickinson. #365, *The Complete Poems of Emily Dickinson,* T. H. Johnson, editor (Boston: Little Brown, 1960), 173.

The Patience of Hawks
p. 75. John Baker. *The Peregrine.* (New York: Harper & Row, 1967), 9-15.
p. 78. Shunryu Suzuki. *Zen Mind, Beginner's Mind* (New York & Tokyo: Weatherhill, 1994), 104.
p. 78. John Keats. "Letter to Benjamin Bailey," Nov. 22, 1817, in *English Romantic Writers,* David Perkins, editor (New York: Harcourt-Brace-Jovanovich, 1967), 1208.
p. 78. Robert Bateman. *Birds* (New York: Pantheon, 2002.)

Hiking the Selway at Night
p. 88. Peter Matthiessen. *The Snow Leopard* (New York: Viking-Penguin, 1987), 151.

Stillness
p. 101-102. William Stafford. "Ask Me," from *The Way It Is: New and Selected Poems* (Minneapolis, MN: Graywolf Press, 1977.

Tracks
p. 107. Walt Whitman. "Song of Myself," Sec. 32, from *Leaves of Grass and Selected Prose,* L. Buell, editor (New York: Random House, 1981), 50.
p. 112. Gary Snyder. *The Practice of the Wild.* (San Francisco: North Point, 1990), 66.
p. 113. Maurice Merleau-Ponty. *Working Notes* (Evanston: Northwestern University Press, 1969), 215.
p. 115. Edwin Way Teale. *Adventures in Nature* (New York: Apollo, 1959), 4.

The Parlors of Heaven

p. 122. Sven Birkerts. *The Gutenburg Elegies*. (New York: Fawcett, 1994), 211.

p. 126. Walt Whitman. "Song of Myself," sec. 31, from *Leaves of Grass and Selected Prose*, L. Buell, editor (New York: Random House, 1981), 49.

Creel

p. 138. Hugh Chattam and Dan McClain. *The Art of the Creel* (Ennis, MT: Blue Heron, 1997). With help of elegant photographs, this book gives an overview of the history of creel-making in the Northwest.

p. 142. Edith Cobb. *The Ecology of Imagination in Childhood* (Dallas: Spring Publications, 1933.)

The Circle of Time

p. 145. Edith Cobb. *The Ecology of Imagination in Childhood* (Dallas: Spring Publications, 1933), 33.

p. 146. Walt Whitman. "There Was a Child Wwnt Forth," from *Autumn Rivulets*. Cited in Cobb, p. 31.

p. 148. Rainier Maria Rilke. Letter to Magda von Hattingberg, Feb. 17, 1914. *The Selected Poetry of Rainier Maria Rilke*, Stephen Mitchell, editor and translator (New York: Vintage, 1989), 313.

p. 149. Blaise Pascal. *Pensees*, W. F. Trotter, translator (Grand Rapids: Christian Classics Ethereal Library, 2002-10), 27. www.ccel.org/ccel/pascal/pensees.html

p. 150. William Blake. "Auguries of Innocence" and "Marriage of Heaven Hell" in *The Portable Blake*, Alfred Kazin, editor (New York: Viking, 1967), 150, 253.

p. 152. Owen Barfield. *History, Guilt and Habit* (Middletown: Wesleyan University Press, 1979), 70. I am indebted throughout this book, but especially in this chapter, for Barfield's critique of western science in relation to the evolution of consciousness. His work bears profound implications for the field of ecology and the possible—in his view, vital—reconciliation of science and religion in the quest to activate spiritual awareness. The pivotal work here is *Saving the Appearances* (New York: Harcourt-Brace, 1957)

p. 153. Ralph Waldo Emerson. "Nature," in *Selections from Ralph Waldo Emerson*, Stephen Whicher, editor (Boston: Houghton-Mifflin, 1960), 55.